# AMERICA'S SOUTHWESTERN
# TREASURES

ERIC AND CHRIS
SKOPEC

Jim,

Thank you again for letting us use your image. (page 94) Hopefully this book will lead you to some new locations and the primer will have some new bits of info for you!

-Chris

*America's Southwestern Treasures*
© Eric and Chris Skopec 2010
All Rights Reserved

**Cover Images:**
Front Cover - Painted Hand Pueblo by Eric Skopec
Back Cover - Navajo wall of repurposed Anscestral Puebloan stones by Chris Skopec

ISBN: 1452873291
ISBN-13: 978-1452873299

# PREFACE

*Photo by Chris Skopec.*

Promises of great wealth brought Anglo explorers to the southwest just as they had drawn Spanish adventurers two centuries earlier. The fabled cities of gold never materialized and most adventurers were disappointed.

A lucky few recognized treasures of a different sort. Amid the snow-capped mountains, high mesas and sweltering deserts, they found the remains of earlier civilizations. Massive stone cities, mysterious cliff dwellings, elaborate rock art panels and beautiful ceramics were among the most impressive treasures.

These treasures have fired the imaginations of countless visitors. They are as stunning today as they were when first discovered. They are waiting for new generations of visitors and all you need to know is where to find them. This book is your key to unlocking countless adventures throughout the Southwest.

After concise descriptions of the people who created the treasures, you will find an alphabetical listing of more than 180 southwestern treasures you might like to visit. Each listing includes a brief description along with relevant notes—location, hours, fees and services—plus a rating that will help you recognize "must see" and "nice to visit" sites and distinguish them from places requiring long hikes, 4-wheel drives over treacherous roads or special permissions. For the adventurous, there are also a handful of more demanding sites as well. A checklist of "must see" sites plus location and culture indexes as well as suggested adventures will help make the most of your time in the southwest.

*Photo by Eric Skopec*

**AS YOU TRAVEL, PLEASE KEEP TWO THINGS IN MIND:**

- Some of the places described are unguarded. Artifacts litter the ground and fractured walls totter precipitously. Damaging the sites and removing artifacts are crimes so please leave the sites as you found them. **Take only pictures, leave only footprints** is as important at the archeological sites as in any wilderness area.

- The descriptions, itineraries and ratings provide only general guidance. Road, weather, access and other conditions can change rapidly. Never put yourself or your companions at risk to visit a site. When in doubt, seek information from knowledgeable people in the area.

Our companion Web site (www.AnasaziAdventure.com) carries updates as they come to our attention. The Web site also lists people who have helped with this project ("Acknowledgements") and references to source materials ("Notes"). Both are important bits of information, but you do not need to carry them around with you.

Finally, the list of ancient sites grows every year. The Associate Press broke the story of Range Creek Canyon in 2004 and remains of an ancient village beneath Tucson were discovered shortly thereafter. In 2005, workers in Santa Fe stumbled on remnants of a previously unknown pueblo under the Civic Center. Both Mesa Grande and Puye Cliff Dwellings will open to the public in 2009. We plan to update *America's Southwestern Treasures* regularly and encourage you to contribute to the process by emailing us whenever you encounter new spots or changed circumstances. We can be reached at updates@ AnasaziAdventure.com.

# Table Of
# CONTENTS

*Photo by Eric Skopec*

*Photo by Eric Skopec*

# ANCIENT PEOPLE OF THE
# SOUTHWEST

*Casa Grande Ruins—For more on Casa Grande see page 122. Photo by Chris Skopec*

## SECTIONS

The southwest is a challenging environment. Collapsed trading posts, abandoned farmsteads and rusting machinery show that life here is no easier for modern people than for the ancients. Yet people have lived here for at least 15,000 years. Sometimes, they even prospered.

The first Americans wandered from place to place in search of big game. Eventually, they settled in well-watered spots and laid the foundations of great cultures. Many grew corn, squash and beans. Others grew cotton and tobacco and some raised turkeys. All learned to build homes of earth, stone and wood.

Today, archeologists recognize eight great southwestern cultures. Most changed their lifestyles and disappeared from the archeological record a century or two before the Spanish arrived, but none vanished. Their descendents were here to greet the Spanish and many now live in ancestral villages and pueblos.

Navajo reoccupied large parts of the cultures' former homelands about two centuries after they departed. Apaches, Utes and Piutes took over adjacent areas. Yet the ancient peoples' legacies live on in stone cities and rock art that are among the treasures you may visit. This chapter tells the stories of the eight great cultures.

# THE FIRST AMERICANS

Ancestors of today's Native Americans were the first settlers in North America. Crossing a land bridge from Siberia, they reached the "new world" around 15,000 years ago. The date is an approximation and scholars disagree about the specifics. Some specialists believe that people stayed on the land bridge until glaciers receded to form an ice-free corridor. Those who hold this view believe that Clovis were the first people in North America and that they arrived around 14,500 years ago. Other scholars argue that early migrants circumvented the ice sheets and arrived substantially earlier.

Debate between the two sides continues and you can read the latest news on our companion Web site, www.AnasaziAdventure.com. For our purposes, the important point is early settlers spread across North American and reached the southwest about 13,500 years ago. The groups settling in the four corners region may have been small. DNA evidence shows that as few as six women could account for the genetic diversity among today's Native Americans.

Scholars divide the period before prehistoric cultures emerged into two broad periods. The Paleo-Indian period spanned 35 centuries from 9500 to 6000 B.C. The Archaic period was somewhat longer, dating 6000 to 200 B.C. People of both periods wandered the continent, gathering edible plants and hunting large game. They differed primarily in the animals they hunted. Paleo-Indians hunted "mega fauna," large mammals including mammoth and mastodon along with an ancient species of buffalo. These animals were extinct by the end of the Paleo-Indian period, and Archaic hunters concentrated on a surviving species of bison, moose, elk and deer.

Paleo-Indian and Archaic peoples left similar artifacts throughout the western hemisphere and geographic boundaries meant little to them. All Clovis stone points, for example, are roughly the same size and shape, and made with the same flaking techniques no matter where they are recovered. The same is true of bone tools, wooden artifacts, camp-sites and other reminders of the first people. These similarities tell archeologists that the early migrants had a common or "homogenous" culture. Although they traveled widely, they used the same strategies to eke out a living.

Regional differences emerged only after people settled much of North America. Archeologists call the development of regional characteristics "differentiation," and believe it gave rise to the remarkable variety of cultures found in the new world. Pyramid builders of Central and South America, mound builders in the Southeastern United States, wooden lodge builders in the Pacific Northwest and pueblo builders in the Southwest all trace their ancestry to differentiation from the common core.

As the Archaic era closed, people throughout the Americas adopted more sedentary life styles. Farming became an essential part of their lives and they grew corn and squash as early as 1000 B.C. Beans joined their crops about 500 years later. By the end of the Archaic, many groups relied extensively on agriculture and this heralded dramatic changes in their lives. The people continued to hunt and gather as well, but even limited farming required them to plant seeds, protect their fields, harvest crops and store surplus food. They built more permanent pit houses, dug clay-lined storage pits, and made greater use of local resources. Unique lifestyles emerged and clear regional differences are evident by the time of Christ's birth. The unique lifestyles are the features archeologists recognize in defining the eight great prehistoric cultures.

### FIGURE 1.1 ANCIENT CULTURES

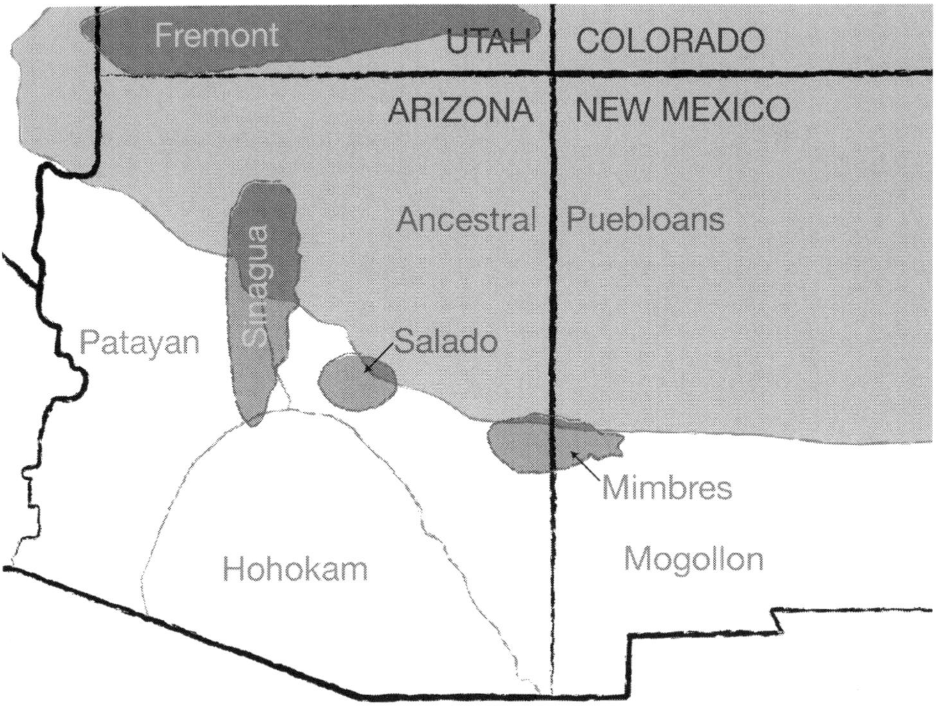

*Ruins of the West House, one of several Great Houses at Aztec Ruins National Monument. Photo by Chris Skopec*

## ANCESTRAL PUEBLOANS (200-1300 A.D.)

The Ancestral Puebloans occupied the heart of the four corners region, an expanse of land where Utah, Colorado, Arizona and New Mexico meet. They were among the largest of the ancient cultures and their monumental structures display the most refined building techniques. They were also the most diverse people and regional centers developed as early as the eight century. Residents of all lived in stone structures, raised corn and other crops, and used pottery, but distinct preferences are evident in and around Chaco Canyon, Mesa Verde, Kayenta, and along the Virgin River.

Early archeologist attached the name "Anasazi" to the Ancestral Puebloans and set out to solve the "mystery of the Anasazi." To uneducated eyes, the Ancestral Puebloans appeared to pop up from nowhere, build massive stone cities and then disappear without a trace.

Today, we know better. The Ancestral Puebloans evolved from an earlier group known as the "Basketmakers." Basketmakers farmed and lived in pit houses much as their descendents did, but had not yet developed pottery. Between 200 and 500 A.D., they learned to make pottery and moved into above ground pueblos early in the eighth century. These were momentous changes, but the archeological evidence shows that other elements of their culture remained largely unchanged.

The 12$^{th}$ and 13$^{th}$ centuries were difficult for the Ancestral Puebloans. Drought reduced agricultural productivity and created competition for resources. A wave of conflict spread across the four corners and the Ancestral Puebloans eventually abandoned their traditional homeland. Survivors moved south and southeast to form villages in central Arizona, hamlets in the Bandelier area and pueblos along the Rio Grande.

The most noted Ancestral Puebloan sites are Mesa Verde National Park, Chaco Culture National Historical Park and Canyon de Chelly National Monument. Others are scattered around the four corners region and the Culture Index highlights many more you might like to visit.

## FREMONT (750-1250 A.D.)

The Fremont lived along the Ancestral Puebloan's northern border. South central Utah was their home "turf" and the culture spread into adjoining parts of Nevada and Colorado. Throughout these areas, the Fremont had frequent contact with the Ancestral Puebloans. Archeological evidence indicates that they even shared some spots.

The Fremont were slow to adopt an agrarian lifestyle and many followed Archaic patterns well into the eighth century. They spent much of the year wandering, lived in extended family groups and built only long term camps.

Around 750 A.D., some Fremont moved into recognizable communities of timber and mud pit houses with above ground granaries. Others continued to wander and some alternated between settled and nomadic lifestyles. These varied lifestyles confounded a generation or two of archaeologists and many referred to the Fremont as "backwater Anasazi." Recent research supports the conclusion that Fremont had a distinct culture and four types of artifact are unique to them:

- One-rod-and-bundle baskets using willow, yucca, milkweed, and other native fibers
- Pictographs, petroglyphs and small clay figurines depicting trapezoidal human figures with large necklaces and blunt hairstyles.
- Leather moccasins with the dewclaws of deer or mountain sheep forming the heel.
- Thin walled, gray colored pottery with smooth polished surfaces or corrugated designs pinched into the clay.

Around 1250 A.D., the Fremont culture began to dissipate and unique sites disappear by 1450 A.D. Most scholars believe the people migrated south to join historic pueblo communities. Today, Fremont Indian State Park in south-central Utah preserves artifacts from a large village destroyed by highway construction. Other notable Fremont sites are in Dinosaur National Monument as well as Zion and Arches National Parks. The newly opened Range Creek Canyon remains partially unexplored and visits require permits along with considerable hiking.

## HOHOKAM (200-1400 A.D.)

Phoenix, Arizona in the Salt River Valley is one of the fastest growing cities in the United States. With less than 9 inches of annual precipitation, it is also one of the driest.

In spite of the arid climate, the Phoenix Basin was home to the Hohokam, another great prehistoric culture.

Around 200 A.D., the Hohokam began farming the Salt River floodplain and learned to irrigate their crops from wells and canals. Corn, squash and beans were their staples and they grew cotton and tobacco as well. Initially, the people lived in simple pit houses, gathered wild plants to supplement their diets and used simple brown pottery for cooking and storage.

In the late eighth century, the Hohokam began trading with their southern neighbors, the Maya. They imported turquoise, seashells and parrots while adopting some Mayan building practices. Mayan influences are evident in pit houses clustered around courtyards as well as in platform mounds and ball courts.

Mayan influence increased during the "sedentary period" (950 to 1150 A.D.). By 1000 A.D., the Hohokam were building walls around their villages and importing copper bells, mosaics, polished stone mirrors and macaws. They also expanded south across the desert and northwest into the Verde Valley. Their influence reached Wupatki near Flagstaff by 1150 A.D. and a well-preserved ball court evidences their presence. Two centuries of relative tranquility followed, but a dramatic change in weather patterns around 1350 heralded their demise. Repeated flooding destroyed most of their canal heads and made their canals useless. Without irrigation, agriculture could not support the burgeoning population and the culture dissipated.

The Hohokam abandoned most of their homeland by 1450 A.D. Their descendents include the Pima, Tohono O'odham and Akimel O'odham, and it appears that the Hohokam became nomads when agriculture failed. The Salado took over some of their homeland, but most remained vacant into the 19th century.

Today Casa Grande Ruins National Monument south of Phoenix, Arizona is the best known Hohokam site and the Culture Index lists others you may visit.

# SINAGUA (500 -1425 A.D.)

As the Hohokam expanded west and north, they encountered another ancient people, the Sinagua. The Sinagua lived in central Arizona's Verde Valley stretching from modern day Flagstaff in the north to near Cottonwood in the south.

The northern Sinagua lived in circular pit houses just over fifteen feet in diameter, grew corn, squash and beans, and supplemented their diet with wild animals and plants. They farmed flood plains and employed some irrigation. Remnants of check dams, terraces and canals are still visible in some places. Their principal cultural contacts were with the Ancestral Puebloans to the east and a few archeologists call the Northern Sinagua "Western Anasazi."

The southern Sinagua lived in pit houses as well as small, two or three room pueblos. They farmed river valleys as well as terraces along the Mogollon Rim and rapidly adopted Hohokam farming practices. They also traded for turquoise and pottery along with woven cotton.

*Wupatki National Monument. Photo by Eric Skopec*

Differences between northern and southern lifestyles disappeared shortly after the eruption of Sunset Crater in 1064. The initial volcanic effects devastated the northern region. Ash buried farm fields and wild plants while game animals died or wandered away. The always small northern population dwindled as people died or moved away.

Just a decade or so after the eruption, the rich volcanic ash created fertile fields and an ancient land rush brought large numbers of immigrants from the south. Hohokam elements predominated and Wupatki Pueblo a few miles east of Flagstaff features a large Hohokam-style ball court. Ancestral Puebloan and Mogollon influences are evident at Eldon Pueblo, a few miles west of Wupatki.

Early in the 13th century, drought reversed the flow of population. The Sinagua abandoned northern centers like Wupatki around 1250 A.D. Southern sites lasted nearly two centuries longer. Montezuma's Castle and proximate sites survived longest, but people left by 1425 A.D. Most survivors migrated east to join the Hopi on Arizona's mesas while others moved as far as the Rio Grande.

Today, National Parks and Monuments protect the largest Sinagua sites. Popular stops include Montezuma's Castle and Montezuma's Well, Walnut Canyon National Monument, Wupatki National Monument and Elden Pueblo. Lesser known sites include Palatki and Honanki ruins and Tuzigoot National Monument as well as the V-Bar-V Petroglyph Site.

# SALADO (900-1450 A.D.)

Around 900 A.D., a group of people wandered into the Tonto Basin near the modern town of Globe, Arizona. No one is sure who these immigrants were and early sites show signs of Ancestral Puebloan, Mogollon and Hohokam influences.

Like their contemporaries, the wanderers lived in pit houses and grew corn, squash and beans as well as cotton and amaranth. They learned to build platform mounds and dig irrigation ditches like the Hohokam and adopted many of the same farming practices. Whoever the wanderers were, they established the foundations of a culture that thrived for over 500 years. Distinctive traits include beautiful polychrome pottery, unique burial practices and adobe walled compounds.

Today, collectors prize Salado polychrome ("multicolored") pottery and it is among the most beautiful ceramic traditions in the world. The earliest version had black painted geometric designs over a thin white slip. The most distinctive type (Gila Polychrome) featured images of snakes, lizards, parrots, stars, the sun, and eyes along with abstract figures in complex, asymmetrical designs. Many designs incorporate a lifeline, a heavy, broad band of paint around the rim.

Characteristic Salado villages are single story rock and adobe pueblos surrounded by adobe walls. Many have platform mounds which may have been elite residences or ceremonial structures. Around 1250 A.D., some of the people moved into cliff dwellings like those of their northern neighbors, the Ancestral Puebloans.

The Salado prospered until the beginning of the 15th century and population in the Tonto Basin probably exceeded 10,000. As the Hohokam society collapsed, the Salado reoccupied parts of their territory, apparently without opposition. Between 1400 and 1450, floods destroyed many of the Salado's irrigation networks and the prolonged drought that followed made it impossible for the culture to recover. Some archeologists speculate that surviving people migrated to Mexico or joined the scattered remnants of other cultures. Curiously, none of today's Native Americans count the Salado among their ancestors.

Salado sites pepper the Tonto Basin but few have been preserved. Construction of Roosevelt Dam (1906-1911) destroyed many and Roosevelt Lake inundated more along with irrigation canals. Today, the best preserved sites include Besh Be Gowah, which has a beautiful museum, and cliff dwellings in Tonto National Monument.

# MOGOLLON (150 – 1400 A.D.)

The high deserts south of the Ancestral Puebloans were home to another unique group of southwestern people, the Mogollon. They occupied southeastern Arizona, east of the Hohokam, most of southern New Mexico and a fragment of western Texas. A good part of their home range is south of today's international border and extends well into the Mexican states of Sonora and Chihuahua. Like other people of the southwest, the Mogollon traced their origins to nomadic hunters who adopted farming shortly after the birth of Christ. Early Mogollon villages were composed of scattered pit houses. They moved into surface pueblos with rock and earth walls in the 11th century and into cliff houses in the 13th century. Their buildings are superficially similar to those of the Ancestral Puebloans, but the construction is less refined. Unshaped stones and large amounts of mud mortar typify Mogollon structures.

The Mogollon's farming practices were similar to those of the Hohokam and early archeologists suspected that their culture was a mix of Ancestral Puebloan and Hohokam elements. Today, most archeologists believe that the Mogollon culture was distinct from their neighbors. Definitive attributes include ceramic deigns, building techniques, ground stone tools, home locations and burial practices.

Between 1300 and 1400 A.D., the Mogollon abandoned their homeland and the culture disappears from the archeological record. The people probably joined other southwestern people in the historic pueblos encountered by the 16th century Spanish explorers. Many contemporary Puebloans believe they are descended from the Mogollon and archeologists see the strongest ties to the Hopi and Zuni.

Apache moved into the traditional Mogollon homeland early in the 19th century. They disturbed few sites and remnants of the Mogollon are scattered throughout the Gila Wilderness, in the Mimbres River Valley and along the Upper Gila River. Gila Cliff Dwellings National Monument in southwestern New Mexico is the most frequently visited site while pueblos in Salinas Missions National Monument have significant Mogollon components. The culture index highlights several other sites.

## MIMBRES (825 – 1150 A.D.)

Early in the 9th century, one branch of the Mogollon culture began producing beautiful pottery that distinguished them from other segments. Many lived along the Mimbres Valley and archeologist named the evolving culture for the area. Their domain included the upper Gila River and parts of the upper San Francisco River in southwestern New Mexico and southeastern Arizona.

Distinctive Mimbres pottery features black paint on white surfaces, but they also made red-on-cream and textured plain wares. Decorations include geometric and figurative drawings and modern collectors prize finely painted Mimbres bowls.

The earliest Mimbres sites feature rectangular pit houses with sharp corners and well plastered interiors. Kivas are usually set deeply in the ground with ceremonial features including foot drums. After 1000 A.D., the Mimbres moved into relatively large pueblos with clusters of compounds or room blocks around open plazas. Each room block had as many as 150 rooms suggesting relatively large populations. Courtyard kivas are also relatively large and often have entrance ramps. Smaller kivas are typically square with roof entrances.

Both early and late sites were typically located near well-watered flood plains where the people grew corn and other crops. Some smaller villages in upland areas may have been hunting outposts that traded game for other commodities.

Between 1130 and 1150 A.D., distinctive Mimbres pottery disappears from the archaeological record. Archeologists believe that members of the culture dispersed into other communities and adopted their hosts' styles.

Most Mimbres River Valley sites are on private land and none are open to casual visitors. Fortunately, many museum collections include Mimbres pieces and the Western New Mexico University Museum in Silver City, New Mexico has a type collection on display.

## PATAYAN (700-1550 A.D.)

Like the early Fremont, the Patayan were nomads. They lived in temporary lodges made of wood, brush and hides. Stone fire rings and occasional lodge outlines have survived the centuries, but we know less about the Patayan than about the other cultures.

Most archaeologists recognize the Patayan as a distinct culture that farmed along the Colorado River beginning around 700 A.D. Their range extended into the Grand Canyon where periodic floods have destroyed most signs of the Patayan's occupation. Wooden twig figures tucked away in alcoves plus scattered manos and metates on the canyon floor are the most durable reminders of their lives in the Canyon.

The Patayan farmed seasonally, but hunting and gathering were major sources of food. It appears they stayed near their farms only during planting and harvest seasons and wandered the rest of the year. We can trace their routes by examining distinctive pottery fragments left behind. From their roots along the Colorado River, the Patayan traveled west into California and Nevada, south into the Arizona deserts, and east to the Gila Bend area.

Distinctive Patayan ceramics disappear early in the 16th century. Archeologists believe the people evolved into the Yuma who still occupy much of their range. The Deer Valley Rock Art Center near Phoenix, Arizona is the only publicly accessible Patayan site in the southwest and they shared it with the Hohokam. Beyond the southwest, rock art sites in California and Nevada may also be the work of the Patayan, but attributions are uncertain.

## CONCLUSION

Figure 1.2 summarizes the great prehistoric cultures described in this chapter. Although its easy to sketch the cultural landscape, its important to remember that the names we use are merely a convenient shorthand. All of the names—Ancestral Puebloan (or "Anasazi"), Hohokam, Mogollon, Mimbres and the rest—are modern assignments. We do not know what the people called themselves and we are not sure what languages they spoke. Each culture was a group of people who lived in a particular region and used similar tools and techniques.

These were not "tribes" in the modern sense of the word. Members may not even have recognized kinship with one another and there were significant differences within each culture. For example, the name "Ancestral Puebloan" disguises fundamental differences between people living in the Chaco region, around Mesa Verde, near Kayenta and along the Virgin River. Differences between them helped to trigger conflicts that contributed to abandonment of the four corners region. Today, their descendents speak at least six distinct languages.

All of the great cultures dissolved before Spanish and Anglo adventurers moved into their homelands. By the start of the 16th century, Apache, Navajo, Ute, Paiute and others occupied their territories. Descendents of some prehistoric peoples preserve their stories and traditions, but the treasures described in the next chapter are the most compelling testaments.

FIGURE 1.2 SOUTHWESTERN CULTURES TIMELINE

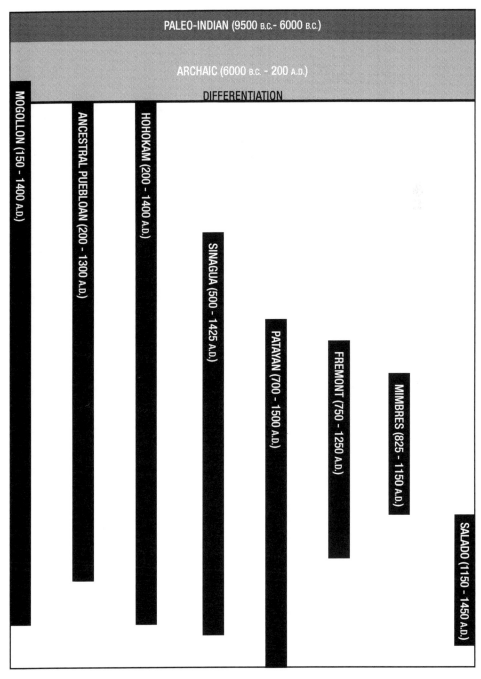

# AMERICA'S SOUTHWESTERN
# TREASURES

*For more on Navajo National Monument, see page 68. Photo by Eric Skopec*

## SECTIONS

Native people have occupied the American southwest for at least 13,500 years. Sites from the Paleo-Indian and Archaic eras show little of interest to the public and are rarely open to casual visitors. In contrast, the eight great cultures of the modern era created stone cities, wilderness galleries, pottery, textiles and other artifacts of great beauty and fascination.

Some parts of the southwest were more heavily populated during ancient times than today and all of the people moved regularly to compensate for changing weather patterns. They built new homes wherever they settled and left a much larger archeological footprint than you might expect. There are so many archeological sites on public land that road building and other construction is a complicated process. In a few areas, there are more than 100 sites per square mile.

Even on private lands, the desire to conserve conflicts with modern uses. Fields plowed to the edges of ancient mounds are a common site in agricultural areas. One friend with a ranch in Colorado jokes that he cannot throw a stone over his shoulder without hitting something of archeological significance.

Of course, not all of these sites are equally engaging. For example, there are 3,654 archeological sites in Chaco Canyon but most visitors stop at only a few excavated and stabilized structures. Sites off the beaten track include ancient fire pits, stone circles, scatters of broken stone, bits of fractured pottery and small mounds.

Still, the number of pueblos and cliff dwellings in the southwest is far larger than many people realize. Archeological databases maintained by various governmental bodies list nearly 100,000 sites and published lists of large sites—structures with 50 or more rooms—exceed forty single-spaced pages. Choosing from these massive lists is simplified by the fact that most sites remain unexcavated. Many are located on private lands and some are closed because they are too fragile for visitation. And, a few sites are in such poor repair that they are hardly worth seeing.

Even after excluding the inaccessible sites, this book lists more than 180 places you might want to visit. Many are in National Parks and Monuments with multiple sites. Listing individual sites produces a modest "double count," but some of the sites are well known aside from the parks that contain them. For example, Lowry Pueblo was designated a National Historic Landmark nearly four decades before it was incorporated into Canyons of the Ancients National Monument. Similarly, Pueblo Bonito and Casa Rinconada have important stories to tell apart from their inclusion in Chaco Culture National Historical Park.

This list also includes a few sites that are not open to the public. For example, Inscription House, Yellow Jacket Pueblo and Snaketown are here because writers often refer to them. Knowing in advance that they are closed will save you hours of driving and unnecessary disappointment.

# THE RATINGS

To simplify your planning, we have rated each of the sites. The ratings are based on our experiences and other visitors have agreed with us. If you find that conditions have changed, please email us at updates@AnasaziAdventure.com.

Three handprints (🖐🖐🖐) designate "must see" sites. Archeologically and/or culturally, these sites are so important that visiting them is essential if you want to understand the Ancient Southwest. Many sites in this category are well developed for visitation and worthy destinations for vacations. They are also places frequently mentioned in travel literature and popular blogs. For example, it is hard to find an article or book that does not mention Mesa Verde and Chaco Canyon, and you could spend a week or more at either.

Two handprints (🖐🖐) mean a site is a "nice to see" spot. Sites in this category are interesting and informative, but not quite worthy of being destinations by themselves. Most sites in this category have pretty well developed infrastructures with adequate signage or interpretive materials. Unless otherwise noted, you can drive to them in conventional, two wheel drive vehicles and services are generally nearby.

One handprint (🖐) means that a site will appeal primarily to people with specialized interests. Most are less developed than those in the first two categories, only minimal reference brochures or guides are available, and you may need considerable background to visualize them as living communities. Services may be remote and many will require high clearance four-wheel drive vehicles. Some require substantial hiking to reach the most appealing features.

Zero handprints ( ) indicate sites that are closed to the public or which impose access conditions that would be difficult for typical travelers to meet. For each site in this category, we have explained why it falls to the bottom the list and tried to give you a sense of how to go about gaining access if you want to make the effort.

Finally, this classification scheme does not apply for some listings. Sites marks "DNA" are typically conservation or research organizations that make substantial contributions to our knowledge of early people in the southwest, but there is little appealing about their offices or headquarters buildings.

As you read the site descriptions, remember that the word, "pueblo" can be ambiguous. In archeological literature, it typically refers to a single building or structure. Castle Rock Pueblo, Lowry Pueblo, and Pueblo Bonito are typical examples. "Pueblo" can also refer to a community or political subdivision. For example, the Zuni Pueblo includes almost 9 square miles with many archeological sites and a population of over 6,300 people.

Finally, before visiting any of the sites, please reread the preface. Remember, road, weather, access and other conditions can change rapidly, and that it is a federal crime to remove artifacts or damage structures.

# ALPHABETICAL LISTINGS

## 🖐🖐 ABÓ RUINS

Abó Ruins is one of the protected sites in Salinas Pueblo Missions National Monument. Walls of the stabilized mission church tower over the fragmentary remains of a pueblo with which it shared the location. Built by the Spanish in their attempt to colonize the area, the church is surrounded by partially excavated pueblo room blocks and unexcavated mounds.

The Abó Ruins are nine miles west of Mountainair, New Mexico just off US Highway 60. There is a visitor contact station on the site along with short trails through the mission ruins and fragmentary pueblo. Please see the Salinas Pueblo Missions National Monument entry of additional information.

## ACOMA PUEBLO

Acoma Pueblo sits atop a sheer-sided 370-foot tall sandstone mesa. During early historic times, a staircase carved into the sandstone was the only access. Today, visitors and occupants enter via less demanding routes, but the nickname, "Sky City," remains an apt description.

Acoma is one of several important places where Ancestral Puebloans settled after they abandoned the four corners area. The Ancestral Puebloans built Acoma in the 12th century on what may have been the site of older villages. They dry-farmed in the valley below and used irrigation canals to water to fields closer to the Rio San Jose. Today, Acoma is one of the oldest continuously inhabited communities in the United States. Traditional architecture dominates the skyline and there are more than 300 adobe and sandstone structures in the village. The Spanish contributed a mission church, San Esteban Rey, and both the church and its graveyard are registered National Historical Landmarks. The Haakú Museum highlights the history of Acoma and its people while contemporary artisans create beautiful thin-walled white pottery decorated with geometric designs. Shops and the travel center sell traditional, hand-made pieces as well as mass-produced "pottery."

Located 60 miles west of Albuquerque along Interstate Highway 40, Acoma is a self-governing Pueblo. Non-Indian visitors must be accompanied by a native Acoma guide and tours are conducted hourly except when closed ceremonies are in process. Fees and hours vary and there is an additional entry fee for the Haakú Museum. Photography is restricted and videotaping, drawing and sketching are prohibited. Digital cameras are not allowed but film photographers may obtain limited photography permits at the Visitors' Center. Food and lodging are available at the Sky City Casino and Travel Center. Other services including a modern RV park are in nearby Grants, New Mexico.

## AGUA FRIA NATIONAL MONUMENT

Agua Fria National Monument protects 71,000 acres of undeveloped land roughly 40 miles north of Phoenix, Arizona. The protected lands consist of high, semi-arid mesas with deep gashes carved by the Agua Fria River and a few smaller water courses. Elevations vary from just under 2,200 feet along the river to nearly 4,600 feet in the highest hills. Wildlife includes coyotes, bobcats, antelope, mule deer, javelina, small mammals and songbirds as well as eagles and native fish in the river and its tributaries.

The monument was home to native peoples for nearly 2,000 years. The earliest inhabitants found homes here during the Archaic Era and people continued to live on the mesas and along the watercourses until around 1500 A.D. when the area was abandoned. More than 450 archeological sites have been identified in the monument and most visible structures were constructed between 1100 A.D. and 1500 A.D. Rock art is also abundant but most archeological sites are in remote areas that are difficult to reach. Pueblo la Plata (Silver Creek Pueblo) is the most accessible. Visitors given to wandering will find other sites along scattered dirt tracks and canyon rims.

Agua Fria is off Interstate Highway 17 and both Badger Springs and Bloody Basin Road exits (exits 256 and 259) lead to the Monument. Neither fees nor permits are required, but

15

conditions are primitive. Roads are rough dirt tracks and high clearance, four-wheel drive vehicles are recommended. There are no services in the monument and the closest are in proximate communities, Black Canyon City and Cordes Lakes. Summer temperatures reach 110 degrees Fahrenheit and sunscreen, sunglasses and large brimmed hats are useful accessories. In addition, rattlesnakes and other reptiles are active much of the year and visitors should exercise caution whenever they venture out of their vehicles.

## AMERIND FOUNDATION

The Amerind Foundation is a private not for profit archaeological museum dedicated to preserving the history and culture of Native Americans. Created in 1937 by William Shirley Fulton, the Amerind Foundation houses one of the nation's finest private collections of Native American art and artifacts.

The museum collection includes about 20,000 artifacts and aims to tell the story of America's first people. Exhibits change periodically and recent events have included images by indigenous photographers, an archaeological poster competition and native experiences in off-reservation Boarding Schools. In addition, the Foundation hosts tours and other events for members. The schedule of events and workshops is posted online at www.amerind.org/events-workshops-tours.html

The museum is located one mile south of Interstate Highway 10 between Benson and Wilcox, Arizona. It is open Tuesday through Sunday from 10 a.m. to 4 p.m. and admission for adults is $5. Children under 12 are free and modest discounts apply to seniors, college students, and youngsters between 12 and 18.

## ANASAZI HERITAGE CENTER

The Anasazi Heritage Center was built to display artifacts recovered during construction of McPhee Dam and Reservoir. The associated Dolores Archeological Project was the largest single archaeological project ever undertaken in the United States. Participants mapped more than 1,600 archaeological sites and excavated about 120 of them. The Anasazi Heritage Center houses more than 3 million artifacts and records, and is among the best museums in the southwest. Many of the artifacts are on display in permanent exhibits and others are displayed as parts of periodic special exhibits. A special "hands on" area is designed to appeal to children but adults spend as much time there as younger visitors.

Today, the Center is also the Visitors' Center for Canyons of the Ancients National Monument. The Dominguez and Escalante pueblos are within walking distance and staff members provide information about and directions to other sites including Lowry, Painted Hand and Sand Canyon Pueblos as well as the Sand Canyon Trail.

The Anasazi Heritage Center is located in Dolores, Colorado and is open daily from 9 a.m. to 5 p.m. March through October and 10 a.m. to 4 p.m. the rest of the year. Admission is $3 per person and those under 18 are free. There is a picnic area at the Center and other services are available in Dolores and nearby Cortez.

## DNA ARCHEOLOGICAL CONSERVANCY

The Archeological Conservancy is a non-profit organization dedicated to protecting endangered archaeological sites. The Conservancy purchases sites threatened by development

*Delicate Arch, Arches National Park. Photo courtesy of the National Par Service*

or pot hunting and now owns more than 325 spots across the United States. Smaller enclaves protect a few acres while larger ones encompass nearly 1,000 acres.

Recent acquisitions in the four corners region include Spier 142, the site of a 13th century Ancestral Puebloan village in New Mexico; Wancura-Johnson, a Pueblo I and early Pueblo II village in southwest Colorado and Puzzle House, a 154 acre site in southwest Colorado with well-preserved remains of major pueblos, field houses and at least three prehistoric road segments.

The Conservancy also publishes *American Archeology* magazine and sponsors educational tours of archeological sites around the world. Conservancy funding comes from donations by its members as well as corporate contributions. There is little reason to visit the Conservancy headquarters but its well designed web site has a wealth of information (www.american archaeology.com/aawelcome.html) and contributions may be sent to The Archaeological Conservancy; 5301 Central Ave. NE; Suite 902; Albuquerque, NM 87108-1517.

## ARCHES NATIONAL PARK

With just 73,379 acres, Arches National Park near Moab, Utah is one of our smaller national parks. Opportunities to see mysterious slot canyons as well as spectacular stone arches for which the park is named are the principal reasons to visit Arches. There are a few relatively short trails, but many people are happy to view the scenery from their vehicles.

Occasional art panels, broken ceramics and lithic scatters are the primary signs that ancient people were here. They probably lived in temporary shelters and no permanent structures have been found. Archaic people as well Fremont and Ancestral Puebloans ventured into the area to hunt and gather fine-grained chert, chalcedony and quartz for stone tools. The entrance to Arches is five miles east of Moab, Utah along Highway 191. The Park is open year round and the visitor center is open daily from 8 a.m. to 4:30 p.m. with somewhat longer hours during the summer and closed on December 25th. The admission fee is $10 per vehicle, good for 7 days. The nearest services are in Moab.

## ᵂᵂᵂ ARIZONA MUSEUM OF NATURAL HISTORY

The Arizona Museum of Natural History in Mesa portrays the history of life in the southwest. Its collection exceeds 60,000 objects from the age of dinosaurs through prehistoric Native American and Spanish settlement up to the experiences of the first Anglo settlers. The collection also contains more than 10,000 historic photographs.

The Southwest Gallery displays and interprets Paleo-Indian and Archaic artifacts as well as Hohokam items recovered in the Mesa area. In addition, archeologists affiliated with the Museum conduct field research and are preparing Mesa Grande for public visitation.

The Arizona Museum of Natural History is located at 53 N. MacDonald. It is open Tuesday through Saturday from 10 a.m. to 5 p.m. and Sunday from 1 to 5 p.m. Adult admission is $6 with discounts for seniors, students and children 7 to 12. Children 6 and younger are free.

## ᵂᵂᵂ ARIZONA STATE MUSEUM OF ANTHROPOLOGY

The Arizona State Museum of Anthropology in Tempe emphasizes research, training and public education. Exhibits illustrate ways people have adapted to their environments and recent examples include a status report on Southwestern Archaeology circa 2008 and an annual Day of the Dead festival. "Isletan Images: A Photographic History of the Pueblo in the 19ᵗʰ Century" developed by the museum in collaboration with Isleta Pueblo is expected to open at the Pueblo in the Fall 2010.

Many exhibits feature Hohokam, Mimbres, Salado and Ancestral Puebloan artifacts from the School's substantial collection. The type collection of southwestern pottery alone has nearly 1,700 pieces, most of which are organized in an online database. Other artifacts come from the 70,000 plus piece collection maintained by the allied Archaeological Research Institute. The Institute is a federally qualified repository for archaeological materials recovered during the Roosevelt Archaeology Studies (1989 to 1998).

The Museum of Anthropology is on the campus of Arizona State University near the main lobby in the School of Human Evolution and Social Change Building. From adjacent parking areas, follow posted maps to the corner of Tyler and Cady malls and look for the building. The museum is open Monday through Friday, 11 a.m. to 3 p.m. during Fall and Spring semesters while hours during summer and winter are variable. Pay parking is available in visitor lots and metered spaces, north of University Drive. There is no admission charge and related services are typical of those found on university campuses.

## ARROYO HONDO PUEBLO

Arroyo Hondo Pueblo was among the largest pueblos built after the four corners area was abandoned. Located roughly 5 miles southeast of Santa Fe, New Mexico, the pueblo was established early in the 14ᵗʰ century. Abandoned briefly around 1345 A.D. and reoccupied around 1370, the site was finally abandoned shortly after 1425.

At its peak, Arroyo Hondo was home to as many as a thousand people. Excavations in the 1970s revealed a massive structure with 24 multistory room blocks and 10 plazas. More than 345,000 artifacts were recovered during excavations and at least a dozen published reports document the research. The Arroyo Hondo Pueblo is now protected by the

*A decayed doorway in the West Ruin of Aztec Ruins National Monument. Photo by Chris Skopec.*

Archeological Conservancy and is not open to the public. There are occasional tours and you may see the Conservancy entry for additional information.

### ❧❧ ATSINNA PUEBLO

Atsinna Pueblo is an 875-room Ancestral Puebloan structure on the Mesa above Inscription Rock in El Morro National Monument. Occupied between 1275 and 1400 A.D., Atsinna's population may have reached 1,500. Residents of nearby Zuni and Acoma Pueblos believe they are descended from residents of Atsinna.

Partially excavated walls at Atsinna stand as tall as two stories and both circular and square kivas are evident. Reaching the site requires a two-mile hike with a 250 foot elevation gain. The sandstone surface in some areas is uneven and this is a moderately strenuous hike. Spectacular views of the Zuni Mountains, volcanic craters and the El Morro valley as well as the Pueblo more than repay the effort.

Atsinna Pueblo is located in El Morro National Monument. Please see the Monument entry for directions and additional information.

### ❧❧ AZTEC RUINS NATIONAL MONUMENT

Aztec Ruins National Monument protects the core of a community that rivaled Chaco Canyon. Great Pueblos built in the Chacoan tradition were occupied beginning in the early 1100s. As Chacoan influence waned, local people modified Aztec and occupancy continued until around 1275 A.D. Only one of the great houses at Aztec, the West Ruin, is open to visitors. Earl Morris excavated the structure in the 1920s and his work makes it possible for visitors to walk through and around the pueblo. Rooms sealed with Plexiglas panels show what the interior looked like when Morris began work. Stops along the trail include a unique tri-wall structure and a reconstructed great kiva.

During the summer, rangers and interpreters present informal talks on various aspects of Puebloan life and conduct guided tours. An informative self-guided tour booklet is also available. The museum displays artifacts recovered by Morris as well as a few items from neighboring sites.

The Monument is located in Aztec, New Mexico and there is a modest entry fee. The Monument is open from 8 a.m. to 6 p.m. during the summer, and closes an hour earlier during the rest of the year. It is closed on January first, Thanksgiving Day, and December 25th. There are no services at the Monument, but most are available in the community of Aztec and in nearby Bloomfield and Farmington.

## ꙮ ꙮ ꙮ BALCONY HOUSE

Balcony House is one of the most engaging sites in Mesa Verde National Park. With 40 rooms, Balcony House is a mid-sized structure, but it is located in a picturesque niche and visitors can walk through the heart of the dwelling. Tree ring dates indicate that it was built in a relatively short period of time, roughly 1190 to 1206 A.D., and occupied during the final decades of the Ancestral Puebloans' stay.

Today, Balcony House can be visited only on ranger-guided tours. The tours are relatively demanding and require climbing a 32-foot ladder, crawling through a tunnel and exiting up an open rock face with two ladders. People with heart, respiratory or leg problems are strongly discouraged from joining this tour. Reservations and an additional fee are required for the Balcony House tour. Please see the Mesa Verde National Park entry for directions and additional information.

## ꙮ ꙮ ꙮ BANDELIER NATIONAL MONUMENT

Bandelier National Monument protects over 4,500 archeological sites in 32,800 acres. An additional 6,500 sites are known to exist within 25 miles of the park headquarters. The region was colonized shortly after 1100 A.D. and ceramic evidence suggests that most residents were refugees from declining centers elsewhere in the Ancestral Puebloan world. People from Chaco, Mesa Verde and other abandoned centers lived here peacefully for almost 400 years before moving on around 1600 A.D.

Bandelier is renowned for the number and variety of preserved sites. Rock shelters, kivas, dams, terraces, quarries, reservoirs, rock art panels and pueblos are all here along with cavitate structures formed by carving rooms into hillsides. Structured trails make it easy to visit a representative sample in an afternoon, but many visitors spend much more time. From the Visitors' Center, the Main Loop Trail guides you past a series of excavated sites on the floor of Frijoles Canyon. Along the trail, you will see a large kiva, Tyuonyi Pueblo, the remains of cavitate structures and the partially reconstructed Long House cliff dwellings. Somewhat longer trails in the vicinity take you up to the mesa tops or down to the Rio Grande. At the detached Tsankawi unit, a 1.5-mile walk along a mesa gives you the opportunity to visit cavitate structures, petroglyphs, and the Tsankawi Pueblo. In addition, more than 70 miles of backcountry trails are available for all-day excursions or

*Long House at Bandelier National Monument. National Park Service photo by Sally King*

overnight expeditions. Caring rangers at the Visitors' Center are pleased to help you select hikes that match your schedule, interests, and abilities.

Bandelier is approximately 45 miles north, northeast of Albuquerque and 20 miles west of Santa Fe, New Mexico. The park is open from dawn to dusk year round except December 25th and January 1st. Visitors' Center hours vary with the season, opening at 8 a.m. during summer and winter and 9 a.m. the rest of the year. It closes at 4:30 p.m. during the winter, 5:30 p.m. spring and fall, and 6 p.m. during the summer. The entrance fee is $12 for a single-family car (good for seven days) and camping is available for $12 a night. Lodging and other services abound in proximate communities including Los Alamos, White Rock, Espanola and Santa Fe. Backcountry camping and wilderness permits are free, but must be obtained at the Visitors' Center during operating hours.

## 🖐🖐 BANDERA CRATER RUINS

Adjacent to El Malpais Monument, the Bandera Ice Cave is a privately owned concession catering to tourists interested in the unique lava flows. A trail leads from the Visitors Center/Trading Post to the "ice cave," a naturally insulated lava tube while another trail offers views of lava flows dated to around 8000 B.C.

Two features may attract visitors interested in ancient peoples of the southwest. First, circular stacks of rock near the mouth of the ice cave are remains of Ancestral Puebloan pit houses. Second, the Trading Post displays artifacts recovered in the area and deals in jewelry, pottery, rugs and contemporary Indian art work.

The Bandera Crater and Ice Cave are along New Mexico Highway 53 about 25 miles southwest of Grants. The concession is open year round from 8 a.m. until an hour before sunset. The admission fee is $8 per adult.

*Betatakin. Photo by Eric Skopec*

### ✌✌ BESH-BA-GOWAH ARCHAEOLOGICAL PARK

Two distinct groups of people lived at Besh-Ba-Gowah and the Archeological Park preserves remnants of both. Around 900 A.D., people affiliated with the Hohokam built pit houses on the site and occupied the area for nearly 200 years. A century after they departed, the Salado built a pueblo on the site and lived here until shortly after 1400 A.D.

Today, much of the pueblo has been reconstructed. A paved trail leads through the site and visitors are invited to enter the rooms, climb ladders into the upper stories, and view artifacts that were part of the people's daily lives. In addition, the museum houses a large collection of Salado pottery, tools, clothing and other artifacts recovered during excavations. A modern ethnobotanical garden shows how the Salado used native plants.

Besh-Ba-Gowah Archeological Park is located near US Highway 60 in Globe, Arizona. Exit the Highway at Broad St. and turn right on Jess Hayes Road. Frequent signs mark the way and the ruins are open 8 a.m. to 5 p.m. daily. There is a modest entry fee, a picnic area is located near the Park entrance, and services are readily available in Globe.

### ✌ BETATAKIN

Betatakin is one of the best-preserved and most picturesque cliff houses in the southwest. Built in the mid 13$^{th}$ century, Betatakin had at least 135 rooms and two kivas with a population of about 100. It was abandoned by 1300 A.D., but remains about 65% intact in spite of occasional rock falls from the ceiling.

Today, you can visit Betatakin only on ranger-guided hikes. "Moderately strenuous" is a good description of the hike. It begins at 7,300 feet above sea level, drops 700 feet to the canyon floor and returns to the starting point. On the floor of the canyon, hikers pass through a gate and visit a close overlook. Until recently, visitors were allowed to enter the site, but that portion of the hike was closed in 2000. The round trip is just over five miles and most visitors complete it in three to five hours. Hikers need to be in good physical condition and those with knee, heart or respiratory problems are strongly discouraged from attempting it. Groups are limited to 25 people and schedules vary with the seasons and weather conditions. There are occasional drop-in opportunities, but you should call ahead for reservations (928) 672-2700.

Betatakin is part of Navajo National Monument and you can see the main entry for directions and additional information.

## ✤✤ BRAZALETES PUEBLO SITE

The Brazaletes Pueblo Site near Carefree, Arizona preserves the remains of a large pueblo occupied roughly 1100 to 1400 A.D. Excavations revealed a large multistory structure with as many as 120 rooms.

Year round water was provided by a nearby spring and the Pueblo sits alongside an ancient trade route in the Verde Valley. Architectural details as well as recovered artifacts point to both Hohokam and Sinagua influences, and the Pueblo dates to the period when the northern valley and areas near Flagstaff, Arizona were being resettled by immigrants from the south.

Today, an easy quarter-mile trail leads from the parking area to the ruin site. The parking area is on Horseshoe Dam Road about 4 miles north of its intersection with Bartlett Dam Road. There is no admission fee and there are no services at the site.

Summer months—May, June and July—may be uncomfortably warm and visitors may be plagued by gnats.

## BROKEN K PUEBLO

Broken K Pueblo near Snowflake, Arizona is the remnant of an Ancestral Puebloan structure excavated in the 1960s. The rectangular stone buildings had roughly 100 rooms in a single story and was occupied from around 1150 to 1280 A.D.

Recovered artifacts include ground stone implements, projectile points, shell beads, bone tools and ornaments, pottery vessels and miniature bowls.

Broken K Pueblo was acquired by the Archeological Conservancy in 2006 and is not open to the public.

## ✤✤ BUCKHORN WASH ROCK ART SITE

Buckhorn Wash in south central Utah is a dramatic gash carved into the San Raphael Swell. Some parts form a steep walled canyon and Native Americans have painted figures on cliff faces for at least three millennia.

Most glyphs are painted in the Barrier Canyon style and include ghostly figures similar to those in the Great Gallery of Horseshoe Canyon. The Bureau of Land Management interpretive site brochure highlights several features and attempts to explain the significance of the rock art. The easy trail to the cliff face is suitable for children.

Buckhorn Wash is easily accessed from Interstate 70 at exit 129. There is a large parking area and restrooms, but no other services at the site. There is no admission fee.

## ᕙᕙ BUTLER WASH RUINS

Butler Wash near Blanding, Utah contains a number of Ancestral Puebloan sites of which the Ballroom Cave complex is the most impressive. Occupied during the 13th century, the site has been stabilized and partially reconstructed. In addition to living and storage rooms, three Mesa Verde style and one Kayenta style kivas are visible.

A well-developed overlook with interpretive signage is an easy one-mile round trip hike from the parking area. The relatively easy trail crosses slickrock and washes, but is well signed and easy to follow. Plan on about an hour for the hike and bring binoculars and long camera lenses.

More adventurous visitors can enter the ruins and examine other sites along the way. This requires a more strenuous hike of 4 to 5 hours and is discouraged by the Bureau of Land Management. From the overlook, follow unsigned but well-worn trails to the canyon floor and across to the ruins. Please remember that the ruins are fragile and should be treated with respect. A flashlight is helpful because some structures at the back of the cave are almost always in deep shade. Although the hike is usually described as moderately strenuous, there are several hazards along the way and this is an "at your own risk" hike.

The trailhead is south of Blanding along Highway 95. The signed parking area is 11.5 miles west of the intersection with highway 191. The site is open year round and services are limited to descriptive signs and a vault toilet. There is no admission fee.

## ᕙᕙᕙ CANYON DE CHELLY NATIONAL MONUMENT

Canyon de Chelly (pronounced "d'SHAY") has spectacular scenery in addition to extraordinarily well preserved Ancestral Puebloan dwellings. Beautiful red cliffs stained by manganese and iron oxide rise a thousand feet or more from the canyon floor. People have lived in the canyons for over 4,000 years beginning in the Archaic era. There are more than 3,000 known archeological sites in the Monument, and most Puebloan structures date between 350 and 1300 A.D.

A quirk of fate is responsible for the remarkable preservation of Ancestral Puebloan structures. Navajos moved into the canyons more than 300 years ago and their Tribal Trust owns the land. By agreement, the National Park Service manages the Monument, but a living Navajo community on the canyon floors limits outsider access and helps to protect the Ancestral Puebloan structures.

Many visitors limit themselves to areas that do not require Navajo Guides. The Visitors' Center, White House Ruin, and overlooks on the canyon rims are open to all visitors. Reaching White House Ruin requires an hour-long hike each way and only visitors in good physical condition should make the effort. The 2.5-mile hiking trail starts at the White House Ruin overlook and descends 600 feet into the canyon. It is steep in places, but generally well maintained. Less adventurous visitors can see much of the canyon and many Ancestral Puebloan sites from well-placed overlooks on the canyon rims. Overlooks along the South Rim Drive provide good views of First Ruin, Junction Ruin, White House, Sliding House, and Spider Rock, an 800-foot stone spire rising from the canyon floor. Antelope House Ruin, Mummy Cave Ruin, and Massacre Cave are visible from overlooks along the North Rim Drive.

*Canyon de Chelly National Monumet. Photo by Eric Skopec*

Driving the north and south rims and hiking to White House will occupy a full day. With more time, visitors with a suitable four-wheel drive vehicle can hire a Navajo guide at the Monument headquarters or join a commercial tour. Half- and full-day tours offered by commercial operators take visitors to some of the most photogenic sites on the canyon floor.

Canyon de Chelly is located in east, central Arizona. There is no fee to enter the Visitors' Center, drive the rims, or hike to White House Ruin. Navajo guides charge about $10 an hour and the cost of commercial tours varies. The National Park Service operates a campground near the Headquarters and the Thunderbird Lodge nearby offers both food and lodging. More services are available in the town of Chinle, a ten-minute drive from the Monument headquarters.

### CANYONLANDS NATIONAL PARK

Canyonlands National Park near Moab, Utah preserves some of the most impressive rock art in the southwest. Visited by Paleo-Indian and Archaic peoples, the park area's population was highest near the end of Pueblo III. Both Ancestral Puebloan and Fremont sites are found in abundance, but the most impressive rock art dates to the Archaic Era. The region was abandoned by 1300 A.D.

In 1986, Bureau of Land Management archeologists estimated that a 6,000 acre segment of the park contained more than 125 sites of which at least 80 could qualify for inclusion in the National Register of Historic Places. The estimate probably falls far short of the total. Sierra Club volunteers are now helping archeologists map sites and in just two seasons have identified more than 20 previously unknown sites. Some archeological sites can be visited with a minimum of hiking. Roadside Ruin in the Needles Unit and Aztec Butte on the Island in the Sky Unit are examples. Visiting the most spectacular sites in Horseshoe Canyon and nearby Lavender Canyon requires more strenuous hikes. The round trip to the Great Gallery is 6.5 miles on a rough, steep trail that descends 750 feet into the Canyon.

25

Canyonlands National Park is southwest of Moab, Utah and highways 313 and 211 from Highway 191 lead to Visitor Centers. Visitors Centers in each unit of the Park—Island in the Sky, The Maze and Needles—maintain their own hours, generally from around 9 a.m. to 4:30 p.m. with slightly extended hours during the summer. The Park itself is open year round, 24 hours a day, but Visitors' Centers are closed on December 25th and January 1st. The admission fee is $10 per vehicle, good for seven days. Services are most readily available in Moab.

### ᎳᎳᎳ CANYONS OF THE ANCIENTS NATIONAL MONUMENT

Canyons of the Ancients is one of our newest national monuments. Created in 2000, it protects an estimated 30,000 archeological sites. The Monument is being developed as an outdoor museum and more adventurous guests can find their way to cliff dwellings, pueblos, great kivas, shrines, sacred springs, agricultural fields, check dams, reservoirs, and rock art in addition to remnants of more recent cultures.

Today, the Monument incorporates several sites that were well known before its creation. Painted Hand, Sand Canyon, Castle Rock and Lowry Pueblos are all in the Monument as are the Escalante and Domingo Pueblos, as well as The Anasazi Heritage Center. In addition, the Sand Canyon Trail affords one of the most enjoyable walks in the four corners region. The Monument extends over 164,000 acres and many sites can be visited without stopping at the Visitors' Center. However, first time visitors should stop at the Anasazi Heritage Center to orient themselves and visit the museum. Please see the Anasazi Heritage Center entry for directions and other information.

### ᎳᎳ CAPITAL REEF NATIONAL PARK

Capital Reef National Park in south central Utah is known for its spectacular scenery as well as fertile river valleys. Settled by the first people in the Southwest, most valleys have been more or less continuously occupied since. Farming by Anglo settlers has destroyed most sites on canyon bottoms, but artifacts, rock art and remains of scattered campsites on ridges evidence Paleo-Indian and Archaic visitors.

Ancestral Puebloans and Fremont people occupied the park simultaneously. Puebloan sites are concentrated in the south while Fremont sites are found throughout. Occasionally, the two overlap suggesting a high degree of interaction. Representative sites include granaries, slab-lined storage pits, pit house depressions, rock shelters and lithic or ceramic scatters as well as elaborate rock art panels. The Fruita and Pleasant Creek areas have high concentrations of prehistoric sites.

Capital Reef National Park is south of Interstate 70 and straddles State Highway 24. The Park is open year round as are the campgrounds. The Visitors Center is open daily from 8 a.m. to 4:30 p.m. except for major holidays and typically extends its hours during the summer. The entrance fee is $5 for noncommercial vehicles, good for 7 days and the nearest services are in proximate communities.

### ᎳᎳᎳ CASA GRANDE NATIONAL MONUMENT

Casa Grande National Monument south of Phoenix, Arizona preserves the remains of a large Hohokam village that was occupied for over 500 years, from around 900 to about

*Casa Grande National Monument—Unprotected mud walls erode while the "great house" is protected by it's modern roof in the background. Photo by Chris Skopec*

1450 A.D. Archeologists have documented more than 60 sites within the monument along with more than 300 miles of irrigation canals carrying water from the Salt River.

Today as in ancient times, the village is dominated by a massive adobe structure often referred to as the "great house." Built by pouring layers of mud atop one another, the Great House has walls over four feet think and measures 60 feet on a side. It once stood over four stories tall but erosion has reduced its height. Today, a modern roof protects it from further damage.

Casa Grande National Monument is in Coolidge, Arizona, about an hour's drive south of Phoenix. The park is open daily from 8 a.m. to 5 p.m. except Thanksgiving and Christmas day. Facilities include a visitors' center with a museum exhibit area, restrooms, drinking fountains, and picnic tables. Admission is $5 per person and children under 16 are free.

### ᭙᭙᭙ CASA MALPAIS ARCHAEOLOGICAL PARK

The Casa Malpais Archaeological Park in Springerville, Arizona protects the remains of a late Mogollon settlement. Constructed of dry laid rock, the principal structure incorporates natural fissures and was occupied for about 200 years, roughly 1250 to 1440 A.D.

The protected site covers 16 acres. Highlights include the large pueblo, a great kiva, three masonry stairways, several isolated rooms, rock art panels and an observatory. The observatory is unique and demonstrates the ancients' knowledge of astronomy. The circular structure is almost 80 feet in diameter and all five openings align with solstices, equinoxes or the North Star.

The Casa Malpais Archaeological Park can be visited on guided tours, which begin at the Museum, 318 E. Main St. in Springerville. The Museum is open daily from 8 a.m. to 4 p.m. except Christmas day. Guided tours begin at 9 a.m., 11 a.m. and 2 p.m. and are included in the price of admission, $3 for adults with discounts for seniors and children.

### 🖐🖐🖐 CASA RINCONADA

Casa Rinconada is a large Chacoan great kiva on the south side of Chaco Canyon opposite Pueblo Bonito. At over 60 feet in diameter, Casa Rinconada is among the largest known great kivas. Excavations have revealed north and south entrances, floor vaults, 34 wall niches and a partially hidden tunnel entry. Casa Rinconada is surrounded by several small villages unlike the large pueblos for which Chaco is noted. Many of the small sites have been excavated and three are open for viewing. Identified as BC 50, BC 51 and BC 59, the small villages are crudely built and average 20 rooms apiece. Archeologists believe they are residences of typical Chacoan citizens and speculate that rituals conducted in the great kiva served to integrate the larger Chacoan community.

Today, a gravel trail leads from a parking area, through the small sites and up to the great kiva itself. The trail is just over a half mile long with a modest incline. A self-guiding booklet is available at the site for a nominal fee, and Park Service personnel conduct occasional guided tours during summer months.

Casa Rinconada is located in Chaco Culture National Historic Park and the main entry provides directions and other information.

### 🖐🖐 CASAMERO RUINS

Casamero Ruins is the remnant of a modest Chacoan outlier located about 50 miles south of the Canyon. The principal structure is a Chaco style pueblo with 22 ground floor rooms, as many as 6 second story rooms and an enclosed kiva. The pueblo was the core of a small community and there are numerous "small houses" or unit pueblos of 6 to 8 rooms around it. Other points of interest include an unexcavated great kiva and sections of at least two Chacoan roads.

Occupied between 1000 and 1125 A.D., the Casamero Ruins site is now protected by the Bureau of Land Management. The main pueblo has been stabilized and fenced to protect it from livestock and vehicles. There is a small parking area adjacent to County Road 19 about 4 miles north of its intersection with Route 66. There is no admission fee and there are no services at the site.

### 🖐 CASTLE ROCK PUEBLO

Castle Rock Pueblo consists of the fragmentary remains of an Ancestral Puebloan village built in the mid 13$^{th}$ century. Situated near the southern end of the Sand Canyon Trail, a few standing walls are all that remains of a village that once housed as many as 150 people.

Today, it is difficult to visualize the village that once occupied more than three acres. However, the site tells archeologists much about violence that engulfed the Ancestral

Puebloans near the end of the 13ᵗʰ century. Excavators have identified at least 16 kivas, 40 surface rooms, two plazas, nine towers, and a D-shaped structure as well as remains of a defensive wall enclosing the village. Construction was completed around 1274—the latest tree ring date—and the village was destroyed in a single violent attack in the early 1280s. Kivas and other structures were burned and many of the residents were killed. Archeologists found unburied remains or at least 41 men, women, and children, many with defensive wounds and crushed skulls.

Castle Rock Pueblo and the Sand Canyon Trail are in Canyons of the Ancients National Monument. Begin your visit at the Anasazi Heritage Center where you will pay a modest admission fee and receive a map to the site.

## CAVE CREEK MUSEUM

The Cave Creek Museum near Carefree, Arizona is a community-based museum largely staffed by volunteers. Exhibits emphasize the lives of early settlers and include ranch implements, a gazebo, the first church of Cave Creek, a miner's apparatus for pulverizing ore and an authentic crushing mill. The archeology wing focuses on Hohokam settlements in the area. Highlights include a model of Sears-Kay pueblo, ground stone implements and a recovered pottery ladle.

The Museum is located on Skyline Drive in Cave Creek. It is open Wednesday through Sunday eight months a year, October through May. It is closed for major holidays including Easter, Thanksgiving, Christmas and New Year's Day. Hours vary slightly and afternoons before 4:30 p.m. are the best times to visit. The admission fee is $5 for adults with discounts for students, seniors, and children under 12.

## DNA CENTER FOR DESERT ARCHEOLOGY

The Center for Desert Archaeology located in Tucson, Arizona is a nonprofit organization that promotes study and conservation of cultural resources. Scholars working with and supported by the Center have contributed much of our knowledge of the ancient southwest and the Center's efforts now extend into contiguous cultural areas of Mexico.

The Center's current research efforts focus on the Heritage Southwest Program that aims to develop a comprehensive database of southwestern archeological sites occupied between 1200 and 1700 A.D. as well as early agricultural sites dating roughly 2000 B.C. to around 50 A.D. Simultaneously, the Center aims to organize regional reconnaissance teams to revisit and assess all known archaeological sites while expanding public education to generate support for site preservation.

There is little of public interest at the Center's headquarters, but its well-designed Web site (www.cdarc.org) offers a wealth of information. Online exhibits include virtual reconstructions of the Sherwood Ranch Pueblo and the Clearwater Site as well as Adriel Heisey's aerial photographs of Chaco Canyon and an informative summary of recent thinking about the peopling of the Americas. In addition, the online library includes recent newsletters, occasional papers by the center's staff and a collection of internet links related to southwestern archeology.

*This glyph, found near the great house Penasco Blanco in Chaco Canyon, is known as the "Chaco Supernova" glyph. It is believed to be a recording of the Crab Nebula Supernova which would have been visible to the Chacoan people in 1054 A.D. Photo by Eric Skopec*

### ❧❧❧ CHACO CULTURE NATIONAL HISTORICAL PARK

Chaco Canyon was the home of one of the three great branches of the Ancestral Puebloan family and the Park protects more than 3,650 archeological sites. There are traces of earlier occupations, but Chaco Canyon flourished during the pueblo eras. Chaco's "Golden Century" began in 1040 A.D. and featured massive construction projects. The Ancestral Puebloans remodeled older pueblos, built new ones, paved a massive courtyard in "downtown" Chaco and created a network of roads spanning four states.

The National Park Service has stabilized five great pueblos and a great kiva in the heart of the canyon. Most are just a short walk from convenient parking areas and graded trails run around and through each of the sites. Rangers conduct guided tours during the summer and there are self-guided tour booklets for all of the sites. In addition, four designated hiking trails lead away from the loop road. Hikers can visit six more great houses and three of the trails feature spectacular views of the canyon and surrounding areas. The Park also protects four outlying areas with less frequently visited Ancestral Puebloan structures.

Chaco Culture National Historical Park is located in north central New Mexico, about 26 miles west of Highway 550. The hamlet of Nageezi is the closest community but offers few services. Part of the road to Chaco is graded dirt that is generally passable in a two-wheel drive passenger vehicles. It can be treacherous following severe thunderstorms and it is a good idea to check road conditions by calling (505) 786-7014.

Archeological sites and trails are open daily from sunrise to sunset. The Visitors' Center is open from 8 a.m. until 5 p.m., but closed on Thanksgiving, Christmas, and New Year's Days. There is a modest entry fee. Campsites are generally available in the primitive campground, but it fills up quickly during peak season. There are few other visitor services in the Park and you should buy food and fill your vehicle's tank before leaving Highway 550.

## ✣✣ CHIMNEY ROCK ARCHEOLOGICAL AREA

The Chimney Rock Archeological Area occupies 3,100 acres of the San Juan National Forest at an altitude of over 7,500 feet. Growing seasons at this altitude are short but the Ancestral Puebloans built here to take advantage of a pair of stone spires overlooking the Piedra River. These spires served as a natural lunar observatory and the moon appears to rise between them every 18.6 years. Remarkably, the area was already occupied when the Chacoans built here in 1076. The locals favored single story circular constructions, sometimes called above-ground pit houses, but the Chacoans built an L-shaped great house with 35 ground floor rooms, 2 kivas, and as many as 20 second floor rooms. 800 yards to the west is an isolated great kiva of Chacoan design while the surrounding areas are peppered with remains of local peoples' structures. Archeological Sites at Chimney Rock may be visited only on docent-guided tours.

The Chimney Rock Archeological Area is on Colorado Highway 151 three miles south of U.S. Highway 160. It is open only four months a year (mid-May to mid-September) and docents conduct four tours a day. Admission is $3 per adult. Services at the Visitors' Center are limited but inviting picnic tables suggest you bring a lunch. Neither lodging nor camping is available at the Archeological Area, but services are readily available along Highway 160.

## ✣ CLEAR CREEK RUINS

Clear Creek Ruins is the name casually applied to the tattered remains of Sinagua villages in Arizona's Clear Creek Wilderness. With a total of 15,238 acres, the Wilderness Area stretches over 20 miles west to east from the Verde Valley up to the Mogollon Rim. Elevations vary from 3,700 feet to over 6,800 feet, and hiking, camping and nature viewing are its primary attractions. There are also numerous archeological sites in the area.

The canyon at the heart of the Wilderness Area varies from a half to just about two miles wide and side walls are as high as 1,000 feet. A year round stream flows through the canyon and there was a substantial Sinagua population in the area. None of the archeological sites is adequately protected and all show the effects of uncontrolled visitation. Many have been reduced to piles of rubble, but the canyon is a wonderful area to explore. Village sites, shattered pots, broken tools and other artifacts can be found throughout the area. The area is an outdoor museum and you are free to examine your finds before returning them to the spots where they have rested for nearly 800 years.

Most local visitors enter the Wilderness Area from spots on the western edge. From Camp Verde drive east on State Highway 260 and north on Forest Road 618. From FR 618, a right turn on FR 215 leads to the Bull Pen entry point and a right turn on FR 214 leads to Cedar Flat. Most of the roads are graded dirt and high clearance four-wheel drive

*Cliff Palace, found in Mesa Verde National Park, is the premier cliff dwelling of the Ancestral Puebloans. Photo by Eric Skopec*

vehicles may be required following rain or snow. It is also possible to enter the Wilderness Area from the east end. An end-to-end hike usually takes 6 or 7 days and should be attempted only by experienced hikers in good physical condition.

## CLEAR CREEK, UTAH

Clear Creek flows alongside Interstate Highway 70 in southern Utah. It is occasionally mentioned in archeological literature because it was the site of Five Finger Ridge Village and extensive rock art galleries. Freeway construction destroyed the village and blocked access to many of the glyphs, but archeologists documented the site and recovered large quantities of cultural material.

Today, artifacts and records are housed in the museum at Fremont Indian State Park which also has trails leading to some glyph panels. Please see the Park entry for directions and other information.

## CLIFF PALACE

Cliff Palace in Mesa Verde National Park was the largest cliff dwelling in the Ancestral Puebloan world. Situated in an alcove roughly 100 feet below the overhanging mesa, Cliff Palace was occupied during the Ancestral Puebloans' final decades in the Mesa Verde region.

Cliff Palace was built over the remains of earlier structures and occupied throughout the 13th century. Tree ring dates indicate that construction and remodeling took place over a 70 year period, roughly 1190 through 1260 A.D. It was abandoned by 1300 A.D. along with the other Ancestral Puebloan structures in the region.

Cliff palace was one of the first major sites excavated at Mesa Verde, but recent research continues to shed light on the people who lived here. With 150 rooms and 23 kivas, Cliff Palace was bisected by walls with no connecting doorways. Archaeologists believe that two distinct communities occupied the niche and that the central kiva was the only place they came together.

Today, Cliff Palace can be visited only on ranger-guided tours. Reservations are required and an additional fee is charged for the tour. Participants must be able to descend into the canyon on a steep trail and climb five 8-foot ladders. People with heart, respiratory or leg problems are strongly discouraged. Please see the Mesa Verde National Park entry for directions and additional information.

## CLOVER RUIN

Clover Ruin is the remnant of a seasonal camp adjacent to the Williams District Ranger Station in Williams, Arizona. Occupied briefly, the village was built around 900 A.D. and is typical of the small Ancestral Puebloan (Cohina) sites in the area.

Today, the site has been mapped, rock outlines mark rooms and portions are being reconstructed. An interpretive sign explains the layout of the village, but like most of the seasonal camps of the era, only small piles of rubble were visible prior to excavations.

From downtown Williams, drive west on Railroad Avenue for one mile and turn left at the top of the hill before the Interstate Highway 40 onramp. Stay on the frontage road and turn left at the Ranger District administrative site. Turn right and park at the old office building. There are no services at the site and there is no fee to visit.

Coincidentally, the William District Ranger Station was built by the Civilian Conservation Corps and is also a historic structure.

## ᗯ ᗯ COCHITI PUEBLO

Cochiti Pueblo near Albuquerque, New Mexico occupies 53,779 acres of reservation land. Much of it is available for recreational activities including camping, boating and hiking as well as golf on one of the nation's top 25 public courses.

Large Ancestral Puebloan communities were established in the area during the 14th and 15th centuries, but living traditions command more attention than archeological sites. Visitors are welcome at many public ceremonies, conducted during June, July and August. Residents have revived traditional crafts and the Pueblo is noted for its pottery, jewelry and drums.

The Pueblo is located about 55 miles north of Albuquerque. Drive Interstate 25 north to exit 259 and north on New Mexico 22. There is no fee to enter the Pueblo, but sketching, audio recording, and photography are prohibited, as is the use of cellular phones. In addition, visitors should not enter ceremonial buildings or other structures without permission.

## ᗯ COMB RIDGE

Comb Ridge in southeastern Utah is a 120 mile long sandstone slab tilted upward at a 20 degree angle. Local history maintains that it was named for an early surveyor. A more popular suggestion is that the name comes from eroded clefts giving the Ridge a comb-like appearance. Although there are primitive roads for high clearance, four wheel drive vehicles on either side, the Ridge itself is a designated no-vehicle area set aside to protect its archeological resources. The area is noted for abrupt weather changes and only experienced hikers with current topographic maps should venture in without a professional guide.

In spite of the harsh environment, Ancestral Puebloans lived along the Ridge and used its natural resources. Paleo-Indian and Archaic sites are present as well, but most recognizable sites date to the 13th century when the Ancestral Puebloans reached their greatest geographic expansion. A few sites are signed to minimize inadvertent damage, but most are evident only to people with practiced eyes and good background knowledge. Please remember that it is a crime to damage structures or remove artifacts.

The closest services are in Blanding and Bluff, Utah or Kayenta, Arizona. Guided tours are the best way to acquaint yourself with Comb Ridge and Far Out Expeditions (http://faroutexpeditions.com/) has extensive experience guiding visitors in the area. You may find other guides on the Utah Guides and Outfitters Web site (http://www.utah-adventures.com/southeast.htm).

## ᗯ ᗯ CORONADO STATE MONUMENT

The Coronado State Monument preserves the partially reconstructed ruins of Kuaua Pueblo. Other sites are more imposing, but none tells the story of changes in the Puebloan world as eloquently as Kuaua. Built by the Ancestral Puebloans as they migrated south, Kuaua dates to the early 1300s and Spanish visits mark critical steps in its decline.

The pueblo housed a vital farming community when Spanish explorer Francisco Vasquez de Coronado and his party camped nearby in 1540. The Puebloans abandoned the community shortly thereafter and decay was evident when Spanish Governor Oñate arrived in 1598. Today, a short interpretive trail leads to a reconstructed kiva and a museum in the Visitors' Center displays Puebloan and Spanish Colonial artifacts along with spectacular murals recovered from a kiva. The murals are among the finest preserved examples of pre-contact Puebloan art and 15 panels are on display. Exhibits in the Children's Wing explain Puebloan and Spanish influences in central New Mexico and the displays will appeal to children of all ages.

Located in Bernalillo, the Monument is just off Interstate 25. It is open from 8:30 a.m. to 4:30 p.m. every day except Tuesdays. There is a modest entry fee and visitor services are available in Bernalillo.

## ☙☙ COURTHOUSE WASH ROCK ART SITE

Several damaged Archaic pictographs line the cliff face overlooking Highway 191 north of Moab, Utah. In spite of vandalism, this site is listed on the National Register of Historic Places representing the Barrier Canyon Style of rock art. You can see large ghost-like illustrations with numerous figures of human forms, bighorn sheep, shields and abstract elements. There are also some pictographs carved into the desert varnish on proximate surfaces.

To visit the site, follow Highway 191 north from its intersection with Utah Scenic Byway 128. Cross the Colorado River and Courthouse Wash to a large parking area on the right side of the road. Follow the graveled footpath a half mile back to the rock art site. There are no services or fees at the site.

## DNA CROW CANYON ARCHEOLOGICAL CENTER

The Crow Canyon Archaeological Center is one of the premier archeological organizations in the United States. Located near Cortez, Colorado, the Center conducts research and publishes reports, sponsors field schools open to the public and hosts educational trips to archeological sites around the world.

The Center is not staffed to support drop in activities, but there are two options for interested visitors. First, a small, self-guided exhibit about Crow Canyon's research is open Monday through Friday except holidays from 8 a.m. to 5 p.m. Visitors can also walk a campus nature trail and visit the gift shop that is open afternoons during the summer.

Participating in a day tour is a second, more appealing option. Enrollees gather at the Center for a morning orientation on the Ancestral Puebloans and have lunch on campus. In the afternoon, participants travel to a current research site to observe excavation in progress. Day tours are offered Wednesday and Thursday during the summer. Tuition is $50 for adults and $25 for children ages 10 to 17. Children 9 and younger are not allowed.

The Crow Canyon Archeological Center is located 1.5 miles north of Cortez, Colorado on Highway 491 (formerly designated 666). From the highway, turn west on County Road L and follow the signs. For information about current programs, please visit the Center's Web site at www.crowcanyon.org

## ❧ CROW CANYON ARCHEOLOGICAL DISTRICT

The Crow Canyon Archaeological District, about 30 miles southeast of Farmington, New Mexico, is situated in the midst of the traditional Navajo homeland and listed on the National Register of Historic Places. Abandoned hogans, pueblitos and rock art can be found in abundance, but the poor roads and unpredictable weather discourage most people from visiting.

Please see the Pueblitos of the Dinetah entry for additional information.

## ❧ DARK CANYON WILDERNESS

The Dark Canyon Wilderness in southeastern Utah is one of the least developed areas in the continental United States. The roughly horseshoe shaped area includes Dark, Woodenshoe and Peavine Canyons. Throughout, steep walls shade the narrow canyon floors and large sections seldom have direct sunlight.

As foreboding as it sounds, Dark Canyon was home to a small Ancestral Puebloan population. Surveys have just begun to map the archeological sites, but reminders of the Ancestral Puebloans include granaries, living rooms, rock art and artifacts. The Bureau of Land Management estimates there are more than 2,500 sites and most remain uncharted. Opportunities for discovery await hikers at every bend in the trail.

Typical loop hikes are just over 40 miles with an elevation change of nearly 3,000 feet. Hikes are strenuous and should only be undertaken by experienced hikers in good physical condition. There are no services in the wilderness area and no fees to enter. Several trailheads lead into the canyon system and visitors should consult a good topographic map to determine the route they will follow.

## ❧ ❧ ❧ DEER VALLEY ROCK ART CENTER

The Deer Valley Rock Art Center in Phoenix, Arizona protects nearly 600 boulders into which Hohokam and Patayan visitors carved more than 1,500 petroglyphs. The 47-acre site is operated by Arizona State University's School of Human Evolution and Social Change and is listed on the National Register of Historic Places. Exhibits in the Visitors' Center explain how the rock art was created and preserved as well as some of the techniques scholars use to interpret the glyphs. An easy quarter mile long self-guided interpretive trail leads visitors through the densest concentration of glyphs and viewing tubes direct attention to items described in the trail brochure.

The Center is at 3711 W. Deer Valley Rd. in Phoenix, Arizona. Admission is $7 for adults and $3 for children. The Center is open Tuesday through Saturday from 9 a.m. to 5 p.m. and Sunday from noon to 5 p.m. The Center is closed on Mondays and major holidays.

## ❧ DEFIANCE HOUSE

Defiance House is a late 13th century Ancestral Puebloan site in Glen Canyon National Recreational Area. Built in an alcove overlooking Lake Powell, Defiance House was discovered in 1959 by archeologists who scrambled up a perilous hand and toe hole trail. At the time of its discovery, Defiance House was largely intact with roofs in place and undamaged bowls containing the remains of food. The site is named for a large pictograph showing three warriors brandishing clubs and shields.

Defiance House has been stabilized by the National Park Service and is located about 3 miles up the middle fork of Forgotten Canyon. It has been possible to reach the site by boat, but declining water levels have reduced accessibility. For directions and further information, check at any of the Visitors Centers serving Glen Canyon National Recreational Area.

## ⚘⚘ DINOSAUR NATIONAL MONUMENT

Dinosaur National Monument is a spot to visit for reasons other than your interest in ancient peoples. The Dinosaur Quarry Visitor Center was the principal attraction but it is closed indefinitely. Remaining attractions include a handful of dinosaur fossils viewable near the temporary Visitors' Center, natural scenery and some fine Fremont petroglyphs.

Rock art is scattered throughout the park and the National Park Service has a brochure with directions to the five most accessible sites. Cub Creek and Swelter Shelter are the easiest to reach and petroglyphs and pictographs can be seen at both. The Deluge Shelter requires a two-mile hike (one way) while both McKee Springs and Pool Creek are more remote sites reached by roads that may be impassible following heavy rains.

The main section of the park is open year round from 8:30 a.m. to 4:30 p.m. (winter) or 5:30 p.m. (Summer), but closed on Thanksgiving, Christmas, December 26th and New Years Day. The entrance fee for private, noncommercial vehicles is $10 and good for 7 consecutive days. The Temporary Visitors' Center is located on Utah 149 in Jensen and the most complete visitors services are found in Jensen as well.

## ⚘ DITTERT SITE

The Dittert Site is an archeologically important Ancestral Puebloan spot approximately 45 miles southeast of Grants, New Mexico. Occupied for just over two centuries beginning around 950 A.D., the principal structure is an L-shaped pueblo of two stories with approximately 35 rooms.

Excavations revealed that the structure was built in the style of Chacoan great houses and many people refer to it as a "Chacoan outlier." Compound walls of shaped sandstone blocks and a kiva are all indicative of Chacoan influence as is the presence of an extended community in the immediate area. Surveys have identified more than 60 Ancestral Puebloan hamlets nearby and the Dittert Site was probably the community center.

Much of the Dittert Site has been backfilled and you will need a rich imagination to visualize it as a thriving community. Today, the Dittert Site is protected by the El Malpais National Monument. Please see the Monument entry for directions and other information.

## ⚘⚘ DOMINGUEZ SITE

The Dominguez site is a small Ancestral Puebloan site adjacent to the Anasazi Heritage Center. Built around 1123 A.D., the structure consisted of four surface rooms and an associated kiva. It was probably home to a small family of four to six people.

The surface pueblo was built in a manner typical of northern San Juan structures. Low stone walls outlined the rooms while upper walls and the roof consisted of poles, brush and mud. The kiva was a simple, dirt-walled structure with few distinctive features.

Today, there is little to see at the Dominguez site. The kiva was reburied after excavation and only low stone walls represent the surface structure. However, the site is archeologically interesting because it demonstrates that northern San Juan people were comfortable living in close proximity to the Chacoan settlers at the nearby Escalante Pueblo.

The Dominguez Site is in front of the Anasazi Heritage Center in Dolores, Colorado. Please see the Center entry for directions and other information.

## DNA EARTHWATCH

Earthwatch is an international volunteer organization devoted to solving complex environmental and social issues. Volunteers support and participate in research activities aimed at:
1. sustainable management of natural resources;
2. responding to climate change;
3. understanding issues affecting the health of the oceans and
4. understanding of human interaction with the environment.

In a typical year, Earthwatch supports 130 projects some of which involve archeological research in the southwest. For example, in 2009 volunteers will help to excavate the Victorio site in southwestern New Mexico. Occupied for over 700 years beginning around 600 A.D., the site was one of the largest pre-contact pueblos in the region. Participants will spend mornings excavating and afternoons sorting, washing, and cataloging data. The expected contribution for a 10-day session is $2,150.

Information about Earthwatch and current programs is available online at http://www. earthwatch.org.

## EDGE OF THE CEDARS STATE PARK

Edge of the Cedars is a small state park that protects six Ancestral Puebloan dwellings occupied from 700 to 1200 A.D. Excavators have cleared and stabilized one of the six, and visitors can walk around the site, enter a stabilized kiva, and overlook the whole from an observation tower.

Neither the excavated pueblo nor the associated sites are particularly spectacular, but the museum is one of the best in the southwest. It is a repository for artifacts recovered in Utah where arid conditions have preserved organic pieces that seldom survive elsewhere. Cloth, cords, sandals and small wooden implements are all displayed. In addition, the Museum displays many ceramic pieces and well placed windows allow visitors to watch conservators at work in back rooms.

Edge of the Cedars is located in Blanding, Utah, approximately 45 miles northwest of Hovenweep. The park is open year round from 9 a.m. to 5 p.m. (6 p.m. during summer months) and closed on holidays. There is a modest entry fee and a picnic area while other services are availabe in town.

## EL MALPAIS NATIONAL MONUMENT

El Malpais is an apt Spanish name for the badlands south of Grants, New Mexico. More recent lava flows are devoid of vegetation and older flows support only sparse scrub growth. Throughout, sharp, brittle rocks make travel perilous.

*The Zuni-Acoma Trail at El Malpais National Monument. Photo courtesy of the National Park Service*

Today, most visitors to the Monument and adjoining Conservation Area are attracted by the barren landscape's austere beauty. Highlights include lava tubes, ice caves, cinder cones, a large natural arch and spatter cones.

Native Americans have lived in and on the borders of this inhospitable land at least since Archaic times. Petroglyphs and small, often indistinct sites are scattered throughout the Monument and Conservation Area. More recognizable sites include the Zuni-Acoma trail linking the two pueblos and the Dittert site, the remnants of an Ancestral Puebloan village dating to the 10$^{th}$ century.

El Malpais is south of Interstate Highway 40 and both exits 81 and 85 lead to the Monument. The Information Center on New Mexico 53 from exit 81 is open daily from 8:30 a.m. to 4:30 p.m. The Ranger Station on New Mexico 117 from Exit 85 is open Thursday through Monday. Many of the dirt roads in the Monument are impassible after heavy rain or snowfall. Current road and trail information is available from the El Malpais Information Center—(505) 783-4774—and Northwest New Mexico Visitor Center—(505) 876-2783. The nearest services are in Grants and there is no fee to enter the Monument.

## ᘠᘡ EL MORRO NATIONAL MONUMENT

El Morro National Monument centers on a natural spring that was an important stop for prehistoric residents and early settlers. People have been refreshing themselves here since Paleo-Indian times, and the spring's importance grew as travel through the area increased. Ancestral Puebloans relied on the water, as did later Puebloans following the trade route between Acoma and Zuni. The Spanish depended on it as well and added reminders of their presence to those left by earlier peoples.

Inscription Rock and Atsinna Pueblo are both in El Morro and described in separate entries.

Located about 40 miles south of Interstate 40 and just over 70 miles west of Albuquerque, the Visitors' Center is open daily from 8 a.m. until dusk and is closed on December 25th and January 1st. There is a modest fee to enter the monument. The closest services are in Grants, New Mexico.

## ᘠᘡ ELDEN PUEBLO HERITAGE SITE

The Elden Pueblo Heritage Site near Flagstaff, Arizona preserves the remains of a Sinagua village occupied from about 1070 to 1275 A.D. The main structure had as many as 70 rooms and is surrounded by the buried remains of smaller pueblos, pit houses and two great kivas. Many walls have been stabilized and it is easy to discern the outlines of the main structure along with the location of some smaller units.

The Pueblo was home to about 200 people. It occupants participated in a major trade network and archeologists have recovered macaw skeletons from Mexico and fragments of jewelry from the California Coast. Ongoing research aims to foster public participation and summer visitors are often invited to observe surveying, artifact recovery and wall stabilization programs.

Elden Pueblo is located one mile north of the Flagstaff Mall on the west side of US Highway 89 north. It is open year round and self-guided tour brochures are available. There is no Visitors' Center or other services apart from chemical toilets placed during the summer. Admission is free.

## ᘠᘡ ESCALANTE PUEBLO

Escalante Pueblo is a compact Ancestral Puebloan village on a hill overlooking the Dolores River and McPhee Reservoir north of Cortez, Colorado. Built around 1130 A.D., the Pueblo has all the earmarks of a Chacoan structure including fully shaped stones, uniform masonry courses and symmetrical layout. Archeologists believe it was part of an integrated network radiating out from Chaco Canyon 100 miles to the south. The surrounding area is dotted with smaller, less refined Mesa Verde sites and the Chacoans were evidently at peace with their neighbors.

Escalante Pueblo is adjacent to the Anasazi Heritage Center and a short paved trail leads from the main parking lot to the site. Portions of the trail may be too steep for people with heart or respiratory problems, but there are frequent resting places and the trail is shaded much of the time.

Escalante Pueblo is now part of Canyons of the Ancients National Monument and visitors should visit the Museum and pay the modest admission fee before walking up to the site. Please see the Anasazi Heritage Center entry for directions and additional information.

## FIRECRACKER PUEBLO

Firecracker Pueblo is the popular name of a Mogollon village excavated by volunteers including students from the University of Texas, El Paso and the El Paso and Texas Archeological Societies. The principal structure had 15 to 17 rooms in a east-west room block. Numerous pit houses which predated the Pueblo as well as many storage pits were located nearby. Occupied through the early part of the 15th century, the site was abandoned by 1450 A.D. and the people probably moved north into the Salinas area of central New Mexico.

Excavations at Firecracker Pueblo produced a wealth of information, but the site is not open to the public. A well-designed web site summarizes the excavations http://www.texasbeyondhistory.net/firecracker/pueblo.html

## FIVE FINGER RIDGE

Five Finger Ridge was the largest Fremont village ever excavated. Discovered during construction of Interstate Highway 70 along Clear Creek in southern Utah, the village consisted of more than 100 pit houses and other structures occupied between 1100 and 1300 A.D. Not all of the structures were in use at any one time and peak population estimates range between 100 and 300 people.

The site could not be saved, but over seven tons of cultural material was recovered. Artifacts include pottery, chipped stone, ornaments and animal bones. Today the artifacts are stored and displayed at the Fremont Indian State Park museum. Please see the Park entry for directions and additional information.

## FREMONT INDIAN STATE PARK

Fremont Indian State Park in southern Utah was created in 1985 to protect extensive rock art panels and to preserve artifacts from Five Finger Ridge, a large Fremont village destroyed by freeway construction.

The Park has nearly 900 acres and features a Visitors' Center, museum and twelve interpretive trails as well as camping and other recreational activities. Many of the artifacts from Five Finger Ridge are displayed along with photographs of the excavations and an introduction to the Fremont. Highlights of the interpretive trails include glyphs

*Gila Cliff Dwellings NM. Photo courtesy of the National Park Service*

displaying hunting scenes, clan symbols, wildlife images and geometric designs. Hand-outs prepared by descendents of the Fremont aid in the interpretation of some panels while others remain enigmatic.

Fremont Indian State Park is located along Interstate Highway 70, twenty miles southwest of Richfield, Utah. The day use fee is $6 and the Park is open year round. The Museum is open from 9 a.m. to 6 p.m. during summer. It closes an hour earlier during winter and is closed on major holidays. Park facilities include the Visitor Center, picnic areas, drinking water, modern restrooms and vending machines. Other services are read-ily available along the freeway and in Richfield.

## GILA CLIFF DWELLINGS NATIONAL MONUMENT

Gila Cliff Dwellings National Monument is located at the headwaters of the Gila River in south west New Mexico. More than 100 Archeological sites are within the Mon-ument and along its borders. They include Archaic rock shelters, pit houses, unit pueblos and Mogollon cliff dwellings for which the Monument is named.

The cliff dwellings consist of 40 mud and rock rooms in six caves. Archeologists sus-pect that the dwellings were home to as many as 15 families and that the site was occupied for just over 30 years beginning around 1270 A.D. Much of the uncertainty arises from uncontrolled looting between the late 1870s and establishment of the monument in 1907.

The ruins have now been stabilized and a self-guided interpretive trail leads to the caves. The 1-mile loop trail is unpaved, rough-surfaced and climbs 175 feet from the canyon floor. It may be too strenuous for some visitors.

Gila Cliff Dwellings National Monument is 37 miles north of Silver City, New Mexico on Highway 15. The route is steep and narrow with frequent curves and the drive may require 2 hours even in good weather. In the summer, the Visitors Center is open from 8 a.m. to 5 p.m. and guided tours are conducted at 11 a.m. and 2 p.m. The rest of the year, the Visitors Center is open from 9 a.m. to 4 p.m. and guided tours are conducted at noon. The tours begin at the first cave and visitors should allow 45 minutes to reach the starting point from the parking area. The admission fee is $3 per person.

### DNA GILA PUEBLO ARCHEOLOGICAL FOUNDATION

The Gila Pueblo Archeological Foundation was created in 1928 at the site of a Salado village in Globe, Arizona. Researchers affiliated with the Foundation excavated several sites along the Gila River and were instrumental in defining the Hohokam culture. However, the Foundation closed in 1950 and should not be confused with ruins in the Gila Cliff Dwellings National Monument of southwestern New Mexico.

### GILA WILDERNESS

The Gila Wilderness is a designated primitive area north of Silver City, New Mexico. There are numerous Mogollon ruins in the area, but none have been developed for visitation. The nearby Gila Cliff Dwellings National Monument will be a more interesting and informative stop for most visitors.

### GLEN CANYON NATIONAL RECREATION AREA

Glen Canyon National Recreation Area on the border of Arizona and Utah is a 1.25 million acre preserve surrounding Lake Powell. Bordered by Capitol Reef National Park and Canyonlands National Park on the north, Grand Staircase-Escalante National Monument on the west and Grand Canyon National Park on the south, the lands of the Recreation Area are primarily desert. Water backed up by the Glen Canyon dam has submerged formerly habitable river valleys.

Only 2% of the Recreation Area has been intensively surveyed, but more than 2,300 archeological sites have been charted. A few date to the Paleo-Indian and Archaic eras and glyphs scattered throughout the area evidence Fremont presence. During the 12th and 13th centuries, Ancestral Puebloans occupied much of the region and they created most of the permanent dwellings. Only a handful of sites are open to the public and Defiance House is the best known. See the Defiance House entry for details.

Glen Canyon National Recreation Area is open year round and three Visitors Centers welcome guests. The Carl Hayden Visitor Center in Page, Arizona is open daily from 8 a.m. to 6 p.m. during the summer with shorter hours the rest of the year and is closed Thanksgiving, Christmas and New Years Day. The Bullfrog Visitor Center in Bullfrog, Utah is open intermittently beginning in May. The Navajo Bridge Interpretive Center near Lees Ferry, Arizona is open daily from 9 a.m. to 5 p.m. during summer months and weekends only from 10 a.m. to 4 p.m. the rest of the year. In addition, there are numerous marinas along Lake Powell. The entry fee is $7 per adult or $15 per noncommercial vehicle and is good for 7 days. Services are most readily available in Page, Arizona.

## ꙮ GOAT CAMP RUINS

Goat Camp Ruins is one of many undeveloped sites surrounding Payson, Arizona. During its heyday, Goat Camp was a 20-room village that served as the hub of a network of neighboring settlements. It may have been occupied for as long as 400 years and was abandoned early in the 13$^{th}$ century.

Today, there is little to see aside from brush and scattered piles of rubble. Things may get better in the near future. In November, 2008 Payson received a grant to develop the site for visitation. Plans call for building a 1.5 mile long trail from the Payson Campus of the Gila Community College to the site, stabilizing standing walls and adding interpretive signs.

Much could be done in a single season, but such community plans occasionally go awry. In the meantime, don't go out of your way to visit Goat Camp Ruins but do inquire locally if you find yourself in the Payson area.

## ꙮꙮ GOLF COURSE ROCK ART SITE

The Golf Course Rock Art Site is a large panel near Moab, Utah. The panel is nearly 30 feet tall and runs for approximately 90 feet along the rock wall. Images include human figures, elk, wolves and bighorn sheep.

There are no fees or services at the site. To reach it, follow Highway 191 south from Moab to the golf course turnoff, turn left to Spanish Trail Road. After a fire station on the left side of the road, turn right onto Westwater Drive and watch for the pullout on the left side of the road, approximately a half mile from the last intersection.

## ꙮ GOODMAN POINT PUEBLO

Goodman Point is a large Ancestral Puebloan site a few miles northwest of Cortez, Colorado. Administratively, it is a detached unit of Hovenweep National Monument, but it is surrounded by the newer Canyons of the Ancients National Monument.

Archeological surveys indicate that Goodman Point Pueblo was the community center for hamlets and small villages scattered across the adjoining mesas. The Pueblo was probably occupied from 1150 to 1300 A.D. and collapsed remains point to an extensive complex with a great kiva, several plazas and at least one multi-storied tower.

In 2005, the National Park Service and Crow Canyon Archeological Center launched the Goodman Point Archeological Project. Test excavations at the pueblo were completed in 2007 and interim reports are online at www.crowcanyon.org. The next step calls for test excavations at proximate villages and is expected to be completed by 2010.

The route to Goodman Point is not signed and the parking area is deliberately inconspicuous. If you would like to visit the site and observe the ongoing fieldwork, please contact the Hovenweep National Monument Visitor Center for directions and additional information (970) 562-4282.

## GRAN QUIVIRA RUINS

The Gran Quivira Ruins are the largest of three sites preserved in the Salinas Pueblo Missions National Monument. The most visible structures include the remains of a 17th century Spanish mission built on the site of older pueblos. The partially excavated church is nearly 140 feet long with walls more than six feet thick. Stone outlines of pueblo rooms and kivas are also visible.

The Gran Quivira Ruins are 25 miles south of Mountainair, New Mexico on state Highway 55. A small visitor center sits near the parking lot and a half-mile long trail leads through partially excavated ruins. Gran Quivira is part of the Salinas Pueblo Missions National Monument and the main entry has additional information.

## GRAND GULCH PRIMITIVE AREA

The Grand Gulch Primitive Area in southeastern Utah protects a large number of Ancestral Puebloan sites that can be reached only by hiking or guided horseback trips. The area was occupied intermittently and many spectacular pictographs were painted during the Basketmaker eras. Standing structures typically date from the Pueblo III era and some have collapsed revealing well protected glyphs behind them.

A handful of structures in the area have been reconstructed and many sites have been recontoured to hide damage done by pothunters. Today, the area is treated as an outdoor museum and self-exploration is encouraged. Occasionally you will find artifacts beyond potsherds typical of most sites. When you encounter a worn sandal, broken shaft, or other item, examine it carefully and then return it so other visitors can enjoy it as well.

The most popular trail begins at Kane Gulch Ranger Station on State Road 261 west of Bluff, Utah. Visiting the most interesting sites requires two or three days of hiking and permits are required. Day use permits are $2 per person and overnight permits are $8 per person. Overnight permits may be reserved up to 90 days in advance by calling the Monticello Field Office of the Bureau of Land Management at (435) 587-1510.

## GRAND STAIRCASE-ESCALANTE NATIONAL MONUMENT

The Grand Staircase-Escalante National Monument protects nearly 1.9 million acres in south central Utah. Recreational activities include hiking, camping, mountain biking, off roading and river running, but there are also many archeological sites within the Monument. Most sites are attributed to Archaic, Fremont and Ancestral Puebloan but none are developed for visitation. The Kanab, Utah Visitor's Center at 745 E. Highway 89 is open 7 days a week from 8 a.m. to 5 p.m. and is the best starting point for visitors interested in ancient peoples.

## GRIMES POINT PETROGLYPH SITE

The Grimes Point Petroglyph Site is one of the largest and most accessible rock art sites in the United States. Located in west central Nevada, the site contains nearly a thousand large boulders on which glyphs have been etched. Human figures along with wavy lines, circles, snakes and other animals are all represented. Nearly a third of the glyphs are carved using the pit and groove method dating to the Archaic Era, about 6000 B.C. Archeologists believe many of the glyphs were carved by hunters waiting for game to come to a now dry lake.

Today, a well signed interpretive trail with frequent rest stops leads visitors to the most interesting panels. In addition, an available brochure describes glyphs at each stop and there are new handicapped accessible restrooms and picnic tables at the site. There is no admission fee but visitors are asked to sign in when they stop.

The Grimes Point Petroglyph Site was added to the national register of Historic Places in 1972. It is on the north side of U S Highway 50 about 7 miles east of Fallon, Nevada and the turn off is well signed.

## ✤ GUADALUPE RUIN

Guadalupe Ruin is a Chacoan outlier atop a narrow mesa approximately 65 miles south east of Chaco Canyon. The principal structure is long and narrow with an estimated 25 rectangular rooms and three kivas.

The ruin has been partially stabilized and related excavations suggest two distinct occupations. Initially built shortly after 1100 A.D., the original construction bears the marks of Chacoan techniques—carefully shaped stones, uniform masonry courses and large rooms. Subsequent remodeling was executed in a less precise style usually associated with people from the Northern San Juan/Mesa Verde region. Stones are less fully shaped, courses are uneven and rooms are substantially smaller. The site was finally abandoned around 1300 A.D.

Views from the ruin are spectacular and few visitors could want more in a less visited site. There is no fee to enter the site and no services are available.

Unfortunately, getting there is not easy and requires driving unevenly maintained dirt roads that can be quite treacherous. To be on the safe side, inquire locally in Cuba, New Mexico. The now closed Cuba Visitors Bureau still has directions on their Web site at www.cubanm.org/index.html as we write.

## ✤✤ HARDY SITE

The Hardy Site in Tucson, Arizona preserves a small portion of a Hohokam village and offers an interesting perspective on development of the Tucson Basin. The Hohokam left around 1250 A.D. and the site remained vacant until the U.S. Cavalry built Fort Lowell in the middle of the abandoned village.

Artifacts must have been abundant because adobe bricks from the Fort contain numerous stone and ceramic fragments. Today, more than 70% of the village has been obscured by subsequent development. A self-guided trail leads visitors through excavated sections of the village where visible remains include pit houses, a cemetery and storage pits.

The Hardy Site is in Fort Lowell Park at 2900 N. Craycroft Rd. Admission is $6 for adults, $3 for students and seniors, $2 for children under 13. The Museum is open Wednesday through Saturday from 10 a.m. to 4 p.m.

## ✤✤ HAWIKUH RUINS

Hawikuh Ruins is a large Ancestral Puebloan site near Zuni Pueblo in New Mexico. At its prime, the structure had as many as 125 rooms in 4 stories around a central plaza

*Heard Museum, Entrance. Photo By Craig Smith, Heard Museum*

with many kivas. It was designated a National Historic Monument in 1960 and the site reflects the fate of the Ancestral Puebloans.

Built in the middle of the 13<sup>th</sup> century, Hawikuh Ruins was one of the spots were the Ancestral Puebloans began rebuilding their society after they left the four corners region. Their lives changed dramatically when the Spanish entered New Mexico. Hawikuh Ruins was one of the first sites Coronado encountered in his search for the fabled cities of gold. He conquered the pueblo after a brief skirmish in 1540 and used it as his headquarters for several months. In 1629, the Spanish built a mission, La Purísima Concepción de Hawikuh, here but relations with the native peoples were not good and priests were killed in 1632 and again in 1672. Eventually, the mission was destroyed in the Pueblo Revolt of 1680 and the site was abandoned by Zuni and Spanish alike.

Today, sandstone rock walls stand several feet high in places and rooks outline the foundations and rooms of the pueblo. Mounds of earth and rock betray the locations of other structures and eroded adobe piles mark the location of the mission church.

Hawikuh Ruins are located about 12 miles south of Zuni Pueblo and administered by the Zuni Tribal Council. You must obtain permission to enter the site by calling the Zuni Tribal Office at (505) 782-4481. The tribal archaeology department at (505) 782-4814 provides directions to the site.

### ❧❧❧ HEARD MUSEUM

The Heard Museum of Native Cultures and Art in downtown Phoenix, Arizona has a world class collection of Native American artifacts. It aims to exhibit the best items from its collection as well as contemporary Native American arts. Ten exhibition galleries are home to both ongoing and changing exhibitions.

Ongoing exhibitions include "Native People in the Southwest," "Every Picture Tells a Story" exploring meaning embedded in symbols depicted in Native American art work and "Our Stories" exploring the diversity of southwestern cultures. Recent special exhibitions include silver seed pots from the Norman L. Sandfield Collection, "Stories in Clay" showcasing the work of mother-daughter teams from Santa Clara Pueblo, and paintings and drawings by Hopi artists.

The Heard Museum is located at 2301 N. Central Avenue in Phoenix, Arizona. It is open daily from 9:30 a.m.. to 5 p.m. except New Year's Day, Easter, Memorial Day, Independence Day, Labor Day, Thanksgiving and Christmas. Admission is $10 for adults with discounts for seniors, students, and children. Free public guided tours are offered daily at noon, 1:30 p.m. and 3 p.m. The Arcadia Farms at the Heard Café features Southwestern cuisine and two museum shops offer handmade jewelry, pottery, baskets, katsina dolls and textiles as well as contemporary fine arts.

## ﬞ HIDDEN CAVE

Hidden Cave in west central Nevada overlooks a now dry lakebed. Pictographs nearby date to the Archaic era and archeologists believe the cave was used as a cache by Archaic hunters.

Guided tours are offered on the second and fourth Saturday of each month and you can contact the Churchill County Museum in Fallon for additional information; (775) 423-3677.

## ﬞﬞ HIEROGLYPHIC CANYON

Hieroglyphic Canyon east of Phoenix, Arizona in the Superstition Mountain Wilderness Area preserves a large collection of petroglyphs. Most are attributed to the Hohokam, but some may date back to the Archaic era.

To reach the parking area, exit Highway 60 east in Apache Junction turning north on Kings Ranch Rd. After 2.8 miles, turn right on Baseline, left on Mohican and left again on Valleyview Rd. for 1.4 miles. Turn right on unpaved Cloudview Rd. and park at the end. From the parking area, the hike to the glyphs is short—about 3.5 miles—and easy along a well defined path. There is no admission fee.

## ﬞﬞ HIGHWAY 279 ROCK ART SITES

Utah's Scenic Byway, Highway 279, near Moab follows an ancient trail along which Native Americans created several rock art panels. "Indian Writing" interpretive signs along the highway mark several sites. The first marked site is nearly 125 feet long and features a line of "paper doll cutouts" as well as horned anthropomorphs holding shields plus abstract and animal images.

To reach the panels, drive the Scenic Byway south from its intersection with Highway 191. You will encounter the first interpretive sign approximately five miles from the intersection and there is a pull-out where you can stop. Additional pull-outs for panels are marked by the interpretive signs. At all stops, be alert for highway traffic. The final panel is approximately 8 miles further and adjacent to the Jug Handle Arch parking area. There are no fees or services at the sites.

## HOHOKAM PIMA NATIONAL MONUMENT

Hohokam Pima National Monument was created in 1972 to protect the remains of Snaketown, an important Hohokam archeological site and National Historic Landmark. Owned by the Gila River Indian Community, the Monument is not open to the public. Casa Grande Ruins National Monument protects the most accessible Hohokam ruins.

## HOMOL'OVI RUINS STATE PARK

Homol'ovi Ruins State Park along Interstate Highway 40 in central Arizona protects the remains of a cluster of villages where the Ancestral Puebloans began rebuilding their society after they abandoned other areas at the end of the 13th century. There are more than 300 archeological sites in the 4,000-acre park, but most structures date to the 14th century. The park is also home to an ongoing research project and the bookstore is a trove of information.

Protected sites in the Park include pueblos, petroglyphs and artifact scatters as well as abundant wildlife. Your stay should begin at the Visitors' Center, which features exhibits emphasizing current research and the bookstore. From the Center, four trails branch out to ruins and other sites. The wheel chair accessible Homol'ovi II trail is the most popular. Just over a half mile long, the trail guides you to and through portions of a 45-room pueblo. Other trails include Dine' Point offering a scenic view of the park and links to other trails. The Tsu'vö Trail is a half-mile loop past milling stone areas and petroglyphs as well as wild life viewing areas. Finally, the 1.2-mile Nusungvö trail offers a more primitive hike across high prairie grasslands.

Homol'ovi Ruins State Park is located just north of Interstate Highway 40 east of Winslow, Arizona. To get to the Visitors Center, exit Interstate 40 on Highway 87 (Exit 257) and drive 1.3 miles north. The well-marked park entrance will be on your left.

The State of Arizona closed Homol'ovi Ruins State Park on February 22, 2010 in a cost-cutting move. At present, there are no plans to reopen the park but you can follow developments on our web site www.AnasaziAdventure.com.

## HONONKI HERITAGE SITE

The Hononki Heritage Site preserves a Sinagua cliff dwelling and rock art site near Sedona, Arizona. The dwelling was occupied from around 1100 to 1300 A.D. and only a fractured shell remains. Parts have been stabilized and visitors can walk through several rooms. Entry to other rooms is prohibited but pictographs on interior walls are visible from the doorways.

Today, there is a small Forest Service building near the parking lot and a modern pit toilet, but no water or other amenities. A quarter mile loop trail passes in front of and through the structure and the Forest Service officer at the site typically has time to answer visitor questions. The site is open seven days a week from 10 a.m. to 6 p.m., but is closed on Thanksgiving and Christmas day. The graded dirt road to the site is generally passable for passenger cars unless there is moisture on the ground and the Forest Service asks visitors to call ahead; Red Rock Ranger District (928) 282-4119 or Palatki (928) 282-3854. A Red Rock Pass is required and you will receive directions when you pick up your pass.

*Hovenweep National Monument. Photo by Eric Skopec*

### ❧❧ HOPI MESAS

The Hopi are direct descendents of the Ancestral Puebloans and preserve ancient traditions. Today, many live in a cluster of villages along State Highway 264 on the high mesas northeast of Flagstaff, Arizona. One village, Old Orabi, dates to 1030 A.D. and is among the oldest continuously occupied towns in the United States. Sites around the village are as much as four centuries older.

Visitors are welcome in all of the villages. Potters, basket makers and Kachina carvers throughout the reservation sell authentic crafts and are pleased to explain their work to visitors. The Hopi Cultural Center and Museum on Second Mesa is the best place to start your visit. A self-guided museum tour will orient you to each of the villages and the restaurant serves authentic food. There is no fee to enter the reservation and lodging is available at the Cultural Center with reservations.

The villages are autonomous units and each has its own rules and regulations. Most close Kachina dances and other ceremonies, and all prohibit photography. Courteous visitors are greeted with warm smiles and rewarded with gracious answers to their questions.

### ❧❧❧ HOVENWEEP NATIONAL MONUMENT

Hovenweep is one of our lesser-known national monuments and only about 30,000 people visit in a typical year. It protects the ruins of six Ancestral Puebloan villages scattered over twenty square miles of mesa tops and canyons. Many of the most interesting sites are accessible on a short walk from the Visitors' Center.

The standing structures date from the Pueblo III era, roughly 1150 to 1350 A.D. At the Visitors' Center, you will receive a park map and Park Service representatives will be pleased to help you plan your visit. With a full day, you can visit a half dozen of the most imposing sites including the Square Tower, a three-story building perched atop a boulder; Tower Point Ruin sitting on a point separated from the mesa top by a perimeter wall; Cut-throat Castle, a circular tower built on three large, irregular boulders; and Boulder House, a large pueblo built on a boulder where you can still see handholds pecked into the boulder below the entrance as well as kivas, check dams, and terraced fields.

Hovenweep National Monument is located along the border between southeastern Utah and southwestern Colorado. The road to the visitor center is well paved and passable in all but the worst weather, but a high clearance vehicle is needed to reach some remote sites. The Monument is open from 8 a.m. to 5 p.m. year round except Christmas Day. The entry fee is $6 for vehicles (good for seven days) and the fee is $10 per night at the campground near the Visitors' Center. Services at the Monument are limited to restrooms, picnic tables, and drinking water, but complete services are close at hand in Cortez and Dolores, Colorado.

## 🐾 Hueco Tanks State Historic Site

Hueco Tanks State Historic Site near El Paso, Texas is named for the large stone basins—"huecos" in Spanish—found at the site. These basins have held dependable water for millennia and the area has at least 29 archeological surface sites along with more than 270 rock art panels. Most of the sites and panels are attributed to the Mogollon, but the easiest site dates to Paleo-Indian times and Archaic points have been found as well. More recent glyphs were created by Apaches and Kiowas while Anglo adventurers have left their marks as well.

Today, Hueco Tanks State Historic Site is an 860-acre preserve set aside for picnick-ing, camping, hiking, rock climbing, birding and nature study as well as viewing rock art. Archeological sites are off limits to visitors, but guided pictograph tours are offered on Wednesdays at 9 a.m. and 11 a.m. during the summer, 10:30 a.m. and 2 p.m. the rest of the year.

The Hueco Tanks State Historic Site is 32 miles north east of El Paso at 6900 Hueco Tanks Road. The site is open daily from 8 a.m. to 6 p.m. year round with slightly longer hours on summer weekends. The admission fee is $4 for nonresidents and includes the rock art tours.

## 🐾 Indian Pueblo Cultural Center

The Indian Pueblo Cultural Center in Albuquerque, New Mexico is a convenient in-troduction to the 19 New Mexico pueblos. A permanent exhibit, "Our Land, Our Cul-ture, Our Story," provides a brief historical overview of the Pueblo world and temporary exhibits display contemporary artwork and craftsmanship. The Center's 2,000-item col-lection includes historic and contemporary jewelry, textiles, baskets, photographs, prints, paintings and murals. In addition, the Center offers traditional dance performances and guest artist demonstrators every weekend.

The Center is located at 2401 12th St. NW in Albuquerque near the intersection of Interstate highways 25 and 40. It is open daily from 9 a.m. to 5 p.m., except major holidays. The admission fee is $6 for adults with discounts for seniors, New Mexico residents, students and children. Services at the site include a gift shop and restaurant featuring traditional foods.

From time to time, the Center sponsors tours of Zuni and Acoma Pueblos. Fees and schedules are posted on the Center's Web site at www.IndianPueblo.com

## INSCRIPTION HOUSE

Inscription House is a deteriorated cliff dwelling in a detached unit of Navajo National Monument. It had at least 74 rooms, 1 kiva and numerous granaries. It was occupied about the same time as Betatakin and a single tree ring date suggests it was built around 1274 A.D.

Largely intact when first discovered, Inscription House suffered from erosion along its base and several decades of unregulated visitation. Its remains are extremely fragile and the site has been closed since 1968.

## INSCRIPTION ROCK

Inscription Rock is the popular name for a sandstone slab at a watering hole along the Zuni Trail west of Albuquerque, New Mexico. Countless travelers have recorded their visits and the rock is named for a Spanish inscription dated 1709. More than 2,000 signatures, dates, messages and petroglyphs are carved into the desert varnish overlaying the sandstone.

Ancestral Puebloan glyphs predominate and they jostle for position with one another, sometimes adjacent to and sometimes overwriting one another. More recent carvings include those of Spanish soldiers and priests, American engineers, surveyors and Anglo settlers.

Today, an easy loop trail guides visitors to Inscription Rock. The half-mile trail is paved and wheel chair accessible with assistance. Inscription Rock is in El Morro National Monument and the main entry provides directions and other information.

## JEMEZ PUEBLO

The Pueblo of Jemez is among the most traditional of the 19 New Mexico pueblos. Residents maintain customary practices rooted in songs, stories, crafts and rock art as well as the Towa language.

According to tribal oral history, ancestors of the Jemez migrated from the four corners region at the close of the 13th century. They established a large community centered on massive pueblos standing four stories tall with as many as 3,000 rooms. Seasonal houses and base camps filled the areas between the larger structures and watch towers monitored springs, religious sites and strategic trails. The Spanish conquered Jemez late in the 16th century and the population was decimated by warfare and disease. Survivors abandoned traditional sites which now sit on nearby federal land and concentrated in the sole surviving village, Walatowa.

Jemez Pueblo is located on New Mexico Highway 4 near San Ysidro. The Pueblo is closed to visitors except during rare feast days. Non-Tribal members who wish to visit should first contact the Jemez Department of Tourism, 74B Highway 4 (PO Box 100) Jemez Pueblo, NM 87024; (505)834-7235. Nearby Jemez State Monument and Heritage Area provides a more convenient way to view Jemez ancestral sites and learn about the people.

## 👋👋 JEMEZ STATE MONUMENT AND HERITAGE AREA

Jemez State Monument and Heritage Area preserves the remains of an ancestral Jemez pueblo as well as a 17th century Catholic Mission. Giusewa, the pueblo, was founded at the close of the 13th century when the Jemez ancestors migrated here from the four corners area. The church was erected nearly four centuries later when the Spanish took control of the region.

Today, little more than piles of rubble mark the ancestral Jemez structure, but it was once the heart of a large village. Many kivas and several plazas have been identified and the remains of the pueblo are known to extend beyond the present day highway and around the monastery of Villa Coeli. There may have been as many as 1,000 rooms in the pueblo.

The mission church is noteworthy for its octagonal bell tower and eight foot thick walls. The structure is composed of sandstone blocks but adobe bricks at its base hint at an older church beneath the one visible today. A Heritage Center at the site displays exhibits telling the site's story as seen by the Jemez people and a 1,400-foot interpretive trail winds through the ruins.

The Monument is located just off New Mexico Highway 4 in the town of Jemez Springs, New Mexico. It is open from 8:30 a.m. to 5 p.m. six days a week. It is closed on Tuesday and major holidays. Children under 17 are free and admission is $3 for adults.

## 👋👋 KANE CREEK ROAD ROCK ART SITES

Modern road builders have followed ancient trails along streams throughout much of the southwest. As a result, rock art is often accessible near roads and Kane Creek Road on the outskirts of Moab, Utah has three Archaic era sites.

The first panel is nearly 100 feet long and 12 feet tall. It features a Barrier Canyon style human figure along with bighorn sheep and abstract elements. The second panel includes images of bighorn sheep, snakes, human forms and a trail that may show a route from the river up Kane Springs Canyon. A well known birthing scene as well as animal forms, bear paws and a snake plus anthropomorphic figures and a sandal track way are elements of the third site.

From the heart of Moab—Main Street—drive west on Kane Creek Road. After slightly less than 2.5 miles you will see the first panel protected by a chain link fence near the mouth of Moon Flower Canyon. The second panel is just over a mile further west on the cliff face facing the river. The final site is another 1.7 miles west. Park in either of the two pull outs and follow the well-worn path down the slope to a boulder with rock art on all four sides.

All three sites are unprotected and show unfortunate traces of vandalism. There are no services at the sites and no fee to visit them.

## 👋 KEET SEEL

Keet Seel (also spelled Kiet Siel) is a picturesque cliff dwelling located in Navajo National Monument. Construction began around 950 A.D. and the structure was expanded continuously until the mid 1280s. It housed about 150 people in approximately 160 rooms, but frequent rebuilding makes room counts difficult. It was abandoned by 1300 A.D. but departing residents sealed doors and windows suggesting that they planned to return.

Today, you can visit Keet Seel only by permit and the number of visitors is limited to 20 per day. You should call ahead for reservations: (928) 672-2700 The hike is moderately strenuous as visitors descend over 700 feet to the canyon floor, walk along uneven sand and stone surfaces, and return to the starting point at an elevation over 7,300 feet above sea level. During warmer weather, some visitors camp overnight but many complete the 17 mile round trip in one day, especially during colder weather.

The main entry for Navajo National Monument provides directions and additional information about the monument.

## ꙮꙮ KEYHOLE SINK TRAIL

The Keyhole Sink Trail near Williams, Arizona is an easy 2 mile round trip hike to the head of a small box canyon. Glyphs are carved into dark basalt faces surrounding a natural water source, the "sink." The context suggests that hunters waited here for animals attracted by the water. Some observers see the glyphs as records of the hunters' triumphs.

The trailhead is at the Oak Hill Snowplay Area about 10 miles east of Williams on Historic Route 66. North of the parking area, a gate permits passage through the fence line and signs point the way. Coincidentally, the trail doubles as a cross-country ski route and blue blazes mark critical junctures.

The site is open year round but the trail may be muddy in the fall and spring. There is no admission fee and no services at the site.

## ꙮꙮ KIN BINEOLA

Kin Bineola is the largest structure in a detached unit of Chaco Culture National Historical Park. The unit totals 1,126 acres and includes many small sites along Kin Bineola Wash proximate to the main structure.

The principal building is a large, E-shaped great house that measures nearly 118 by 50 yards and encloses a large plaza. Today, walls standing three stories tall are visible but earlier visitors reported collapsed walls indicating that the structure once stood at least four stories tall. Tree ring dates indicate that the structure was constructed around 940 A.D. and substantially expanded around 1120 A.D. The site has not been excavated but visible features include two plaza areas with ten subterranian kivas, two tower kivas and a great kiva just outside the couryards.

Archeologists believe Ancestral Puebloans settled the Kin Bineola area to take advantage of the arable land and available water. A steep mesa guards the north and east sides while the structure is terraced and opens to the south. It faces the wash and a broad floodplane while remnants of a large dam and water control system are visible from the structure.

Kin Bineola Pueblo is located about 6 miles off Highway 371 and is reached via a series of dirt tracks. Four wheel drive may be necessary following rain or snow, and there are no visitors services at the site. Staff at the Chaco Culture Visitors' Center can provide a map

*Kin Bineola. Photo by Eric Skopec*

and information about current road conditions. Please see the Chaco Culture entry for directions and additional information.

## KIN YA'A

Kin Ya'a is an outlying great house approximately 25 miles southwest of Chaco Canyon. The pueblo was the centerpiece of a small community and more than a hundred smaller sites have been identified in the immediate area. Administratively, it is a detached unit of Chaco Culture National Historical Park and covers 260 acres.

Kin Ya'a has not been excavated, but surface features indicated that it was a rectangular building with at least 35 ground floor rooms. Rubble piles suggest that it may have been three stories tall and depressions mark at least four kivas. Scattered tree ring dates indicate that it was constructed at the end of the 11th century, around 1080 A.D.

Today the most visible feature is the remnant of a four-story tower kiva. Only a fraction of the tower remains standing but it is visible for some distance and is an easy beacon once you draw close. Archeologists speculate that the tower was part of a line of sight signaling system that integrated Chacoan communities.

Kin Ya'a Pueblo is located along Highway 371 near Crow Point, New Mexico. Access to the site involves driving unsigned dirt tracks and four-wheel drive may be required after rain or snow. Staff at the Chaco Culture Visitors' Center can provide a map and information about current road conditions. Please see the Chaco Culture entry for directions and additional information.

## KINISHBA RUINS NATIONAL HISTORIC LANDMARK

Kinishba Ruins National Historic Landmark is the site of a large Mogollon village on the White Mountain Apache Reservation near Carrizo, Arizona. Occupied around 1230 A.D., the site contains nine large stone structures with nearly 600 ground floor rooms. Archeologists estimate the peak population at 1,000 people and believe it was abandoned around 1350 A.D.

While regarded as a Mogollon pueblo, Kinishba Ruins has a mix of architectural features and ceramic types. The site reflects a fusion of Mogollon and Ancestral Puebloan cultures, a mixture common to the 13th and 14th century sites in the area. Surveys have located about 20 large villages with 150 rooms or more in the immediate area and Kinishba Ruins is the most accessible.

The White Mountain Apache are proud of their cultural heritage as well as that of their predecessors. Part of historic Fort Apache has been converted into a Cultural Center displaying works of contemporary artists and preserving culturally significant artifacts. The Center is located adjacent to Arizona 73 about 7 miles west of Whiteriver, Arizona and is open Monday through Saturday from 8 a.m. to 5 p.m. during the summer. In the off season it is open Monday through Friday from 8 a.m. to 5 p.m. Admission is $3 for adults, $2 for students and children under 10 are free. Guided tours are available seasonally and modest services are available on the Reservation.

## LAGUNA PUEBLO

Founded by the Spanish in 1699, Laguna was home for survivors of the Pueblo Revolt. Although the Pueblo is relatively new, at least by Puebloan standards, it sits amid many earlier sites. Archaic people lived in the area as early as 3,000 B.C., but the population boomed in the 14th century as Ancestral Puebloans moved into the region.

Laguna places less emphasis on tourism that either Acoma or Zuni Pueblos, but the mission church and local crafts attract many visitors. Residents celebrate the feast of St. Joseph on September 19th and village squares fill with hundreds of booths selling native arts and crafts. The rest of the year, pottery and other traditional crafts are available from pueblo members in the village

Laguna straddles Historic Route 66 about 50 miles west of Albuquerque, New Mexico. The mission church is visible from Interstate Highway 40 and visitors are welcome during daylight hours year-round. There is no admission or photo fee, but the Pueblo prohibits video and audio recording. Food, beverages, and vehicle services are available at the Dancing Eagle Casino at the junction of Interstate 40 and the local access road. There is also an RV park and other services are readily available at several spots along the Interstate.

## LITTLE BLACK MOUNTAIN PETROGLYPH SITE

The Little Black Mountain Petroglyph Site near St. George, Utah has over 500 glyphs carved into a cliff face and boulders along the foot of a mesa. Many of the glyphs are

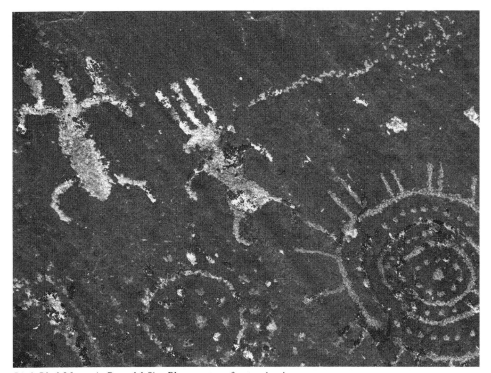

*Little Black Mountain Petroglyh Site. Photo courtesy of www.riparian.smugmug.com*

characteristic of Ancestral Puebloan designs and there are also older images dating back to the Archaic Era. Images include turtles, lizards and bear paws as well as more abstract designs. An easy half-mile round trip trail leads from the parking area to the glyphs.

From St. George, drive south on Quail Hill Road (BLM Road 1069). One quarter mile south of the Utah-Arizona state line, turn left on the unnumbered road and drive 4 miles east to the parking area. There is no admission fee and no services at the site.

## LOMA DEL RIO

The Loma del Rio Archaeological Site in Tempe, Arizona is the remnant of a small Hohokam village occupied around 1200 A.D. Recognizable features include adobe and cobble rooms as well as a paved work area and hillside terraces. Archeologists believe it was home to a single extended family.

Located on a bench between the Salt River and a low hill, Loma del Rio was a agricultural settlement. Residents grew corn, squash and beans on the floodplain and agave on the hillside terraces. Archeological evidence suggest that residents traded surplus food for pottery and stone tools imported from as far away as Casas Grandes in Mexico and the Flagstaff, Arizona region.

Damaged by generations of pothunters and the subject of several formal excavations, Loma del Rio has been stabilized and is now contained by the 296-acre Papago Park at the southeastern corner of E. McDowell Road and N. 52nd St. There is no fee to enter the park and recent additions include a wheelchair accessible path and shade ramada.

*Long House ruins in Mesa Verde National Park. Image by Caitlyn Willows*

### ☙ ☙ ☙ LONG HOUSE

Long House is the second largest cliff dwelling in Mesa Verde National Park. Even though it had at least 150 rooms and 22 kivas, it was occupied for barely 30 years, roughly 1250 to 1280 A.D.

These were turbulent years and the Ancestral Puebloans built Long House when they abandoned the eastern half of Mesa Verde. Long House itself was vacated when the Ancestral Puebloans left the four corners area.

Long House can be visited only on ranger guided tours conducted between the Memorial Day weekend and Labor Day (the last Sunday in May through the first Monday in September), and there is an additional $3 fee for the tour. The 90-minute Long House tour is moderately strenuous. The round trip is only 3/4 of a mile, but includes a 100-foot descent into the canyon and climbing two 15-foot ladders. People with heart, respiratory or leg problems are strongly discouraged.

Tickets must be purchased in advance and in person at the Far View Visitor Center. Long House is in a relatively protected area of the Park and only trams are permitted to drive from the parking area to the trailhead. Trams are available on a first-come/first-served basis and you should allow two hours to get from the parking area to the trailhead. Coincidentally, the tram ride provides opportunities to visit several other sites including the Badger House Community, Kodak House Overlook, Long House Overlook, and Nordenskiold Site #16 trail.

Please see the Mesa Verde entry for directions to the Park and other information.

## ᩘᩘᩘ LOST CITY MUSEUM OF ARCHEOLOGY

The Lost City Museum in Overton, Nevada conserves and displays artifacts recovered from Ancestral Puebloan sites inundated by Lake Mead. Originally built by the Civilian Conservation Corp and managed by the National Park Service, the Lost City Museum is now managed by the Nevada Department of Cultural Affairs.

Hoover Dam created Lake Mead and backed up water over nearly 50 sites along the Virgin River and more than 100 along the Muddy River. Most were occupied between 700 and 1150 A.D. and artifacts salvaged from them are housed in the original wing of the Museum. A wing was added in 1973 to host exhibitions dealing with Paleo-Indian, Archaic, Paiute and historical artifacts. The newest wing, built in 1981, is built over an excavated pueblo and features a recreated excavation as well as temporary exhibits and a gift shop.

The Museum is at 721 S. Moapa Valley Boulevard in Overton and is open daily from 8:30 a.m. to 4:30 p.m. except Thanksgiving Day, December 25, and January 1. Admission is $3 for adults age 18 and over, $2 for anyone over 65. There is no admission fee for children or members.

## ᩘᩘᩘ LOWRY PUEBLO

Lowry Pueblo is an Ancestral Puebloan site northwest of Cortez, Colorado. Constructed around 1060 A.D., the building was home to as many as 100 people. Built in Chacoan tradition, Lowery Pueblo is often described as an "outlier." Archeologists believe Lowry was part of a network of villages radiating out from Chaco Canyon a hundred miles to the south. The area was already occupied by people in the Mesa Verde tradition when Lowry was built and later additions evidence Mesa Verdean techniques including less carefully shaped stones, irregular masonry courses with more mud mortar and a less symmetrical design.

Today, a dirt trail with interpretive signs leads visitors around the 40 room pueblo and to an adjacent great kiva. Highlights include a painted kiva from which excavators removed murals now on display at the Anasazi Heritage Center and stone figures of Winter and Summer People in the great kiva.

Lowry Pueblo was declared a National Historic Landmark in 1967 and is now part of Canyons of the Ancients National Monument. The Bureau of Land Management has a brief a brochure explaining the site and a more detailed trail guide is available online at www.AnasaziAdventure.com. You may drive directly to the site following directions in the trail guide, but first time visitors should start at the Anasazi Heritage Center. The museum will orient you to the site and you can get a map while learning about current road conditions.

Please see the Anasazi Heritage Center entry for directions and other information.

## LYMAN LAKE PETROGLYPH TRAILS

Lyman Lake was formed by damming the Little Colorado River and countless Ancestral Puebloan sites were inundated by the rising water. Fortunately, rock art panels above the flood plain have been preserved in Lyman Lake State Park near Springerville, Arizona. Two designated trails lead to some of the panels.

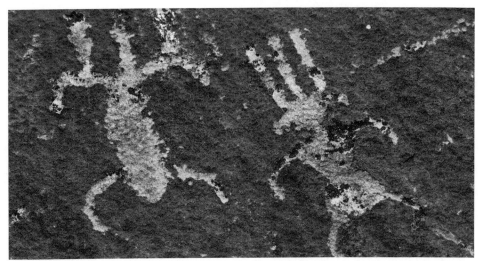

*Ancestral Puebloan petroglyphs. Photo courtesy of www.riparian.smugmug.com*

The Peninsula Point Trail is a relatively easy quarter mile route from the campground. Glyphs along the walk include human figures, handprints, deer and abstract designs as well as a more complex glyph some observers see as a map.

The longer, more strenuous half-mile Ultimate Petroglyph Trail on the east side of the lake can be reached only by boat. The trail leads from the edge of the lake to Ultimate Rock. Glyphs include spirals thought to depict migrations as well as birds, dogs, scorpions and the deity Ma'saw. Guided tours are available seasonally.

Lyman Lake State Park and the Petroglyph Trails are currently closed. Please see the main Park entry additional information.

## LYMAN LAKE STATE PARK

Lyman Lake State Park near Springerville, Arizona occupies the shores of a man-made lake formed by damming the Little Colorado River in 1915. Today's attractions include fishing, boating, camping and hiking but water from the river has encouraged centuries of occupation.

The earliest signs of human activity date to around 6000 B.C. and numerous sites now lie beneath the lake. Fortunately, developers were able to preserve Rattlesnake Pueblo and many rock art panels along two trails. There are separate entries for both the Pueblo and the petroglyph trails.

Lyman Lake State Park is adjacent to Highway 180/191 nineteen miles north of Springerville, Arizona. The State of Arizona closed Lyman Lake State Park on February 22, 2010 in a cost-cutting move. At present, there are no plans to reopen the park but you can follow developments on our web site www.AnasaziAdventure.com.

## MAXWELL MUSEUM OF ANTHROPOLOGY

The Maxwell Museum of Anthropology in Albuquerque, New Mexico aims to increase understanding of the human cultures and emphasizes the American southwest.

With its three associated institutes—the Office of Contract Archaeology, the Alfonso Ortiz Center for Intercultural Studies and the Maxwell Center for Anthropological Research—the Museum collects, curates and interprets anthropological objects. Its collection exceeds 10 million items.

The Museum's two permanent exhibits are "Ancestors," focusing on human origins, and "People of the Southwest," with a reconstructed Chacoan room, an outstanding collection of prehistoric pottery and hands-on activities for children. Temporary exhibits are housed in the North Gallery and the Contemporary Southwest Gallery.

The Maxwell Museum is located on the University of New Mexico campus east of Broadway Boulevard between Las Lomas and Dr. M. L. King Avenue. Limited parking is available in the area. The Museum is open from 9 a.m. to 4 p.m. Tuesday through Friday and from 10 a.m. to 4 p.m. on Saturdays. It is closed on Sunday, Monday and major holidays. There is no admission fee but donations are welcomed.

## MESA GRANDE RUINS

Mesa Grande is a remnant of a large Hohokam village largely buried beneath the streets of Mesa, Arizona. A six-acre fragment containing a temple mound and ball court has been saved from development, but is not yet open to the public.

In November 2008, the City of Mesa received a grant to stabilize the mound, add walking trails and create interperative materials. No date has been set for the opening, but city officials hope that visitation will be possible by the end of 2009.

The Arizona Museum of Natural History in Mesa is responsible for the site. You can follow progress on their website (http://www.arizonamuseumofnaturalhistory.org) or call (480) 644-2230 for current information.

## MESA VERDE NATIONAL PARK

Mesa Verde is one of our premier national parks and nearly 450,000 people visit every year. The Ancestral Puebloans lived on the Mesa for at least 700 years (roughly 600 through 1300 A.D.) and the park contains more than 4,000 known archeological sites.

Mesa Verde has sites that span the gamut, and you will be able to visit pit houses, surface pueblos, cliff dwellings, masonry dams and reservoirs while viewing both petroglyphs and pictographs. Highlights include the largest known cliff dwelling, an unfinished Chaco style pueblo, developmental sites with pit houses and unit pueblos, and hiking trails overlooking backcountry canyons and cliff dwellings closed to visitors. Many sites are open for self-guided visits, but you can only visit Cliff Palace, Balcony House and Long House on ranger-guided tours. Tour groups fill up quickly, and you should reserve spots when you stop at the Visitors' Center.

Located between Mancos and Cortez, Colorado, Mesa Verde is a large Park and houses a museum, several eating spots and lodging at the Far View Lodge. Be sure to book in advance if you plan to visit during the summer months. From late April through mid October, campsites are available on a first-come first-served basis in the Morefield Campground. Additional lodging and other services are available in Cortez, Colorado, ten miles west of the park entrance as well as in Durango and Mancos.

*Montezuma's Castle. Photo by Eric Skopec*

## MIMBRES RIVER VALLEY RUINS

The Mimbres River runs from the Gila National Forest south into northern Chihuahua, Mexico. Numerous archeological sites are found along the river and Jesse Fewkes' classic *Archaeology of the Lower Mimbres Valley* published in 1914 helped to define the Mimbres culture. Current archeological reports frequently mention Nan Ranch, Swarts Ruin and the Disert Site along the river.

Unfortunately, none of the sites have been developed for visitation. Most of them are on private land and none are open to tourists.

## MITCHELL SPRINGS RUIN GROUP

The Mitchell Springs Ruin Group is a private 1,079-acre preserve near Cortez, Colorado. A large Ancestral Puebloan village occupied the site and although some structures have been partially excavated, most remain undisturbed.

The site was continuously occupied for over 500 years, from Basketmaker III through the end of the 13th century. Surface surveys indicate that pueblos on the site housed a population approaching 1,000 people in 300 rooms with as many as 35 kivas. Recent tests with ground penetrating radar have identified an additional 20 kivas and an isolated great kiva on nearby ridges.

The Mitchell Springs Ruin Group is privately owned and not open to the public. Occasional private tours can be arranged when excavations are in progress. For details, you may call (970) 565-8760.

## MONTEZUMA'S CASTLE

Montezuma's Castle is a spectacular Sinagua cliff dwelling in Arizona's Verde Valley. Built around 1125 A.D. and occupied until 1425, the Castle sits in a high alcove above the

Beaver Creek flood plain. The Castle has 19 rooms in five stories and probably housed 45 to 50 people. There is also evidence of a collapsed pueblo at the base of the cliff.

Today, a well-appointed Visitors' Center is the first stop on a tour of Montezuma's Castle. Informative displays explain the Sinagua lifestyle and the role of the Castle. There are also restrooms, drinking fountains and a small bookstore. From the Visitors' Center, a level paved trail leads along the base of the cliff and circles back. Many photographers line the fence at the base of the cliff but you may find more engaging shots further along the circle.

Montezuma's Castle is 5 miles north of Camp Verde, Arizona and there is a well-signed exit from Interstate Highway 17 (exit 289). The monument is open daily from 8 a.m. to 5 p.m. (winter) or 6 p.m. (summer) but closed on Christmas Day. Admission is $5 and children under 16 are free. Additional services are available in several small communities along Interstate Highway 17.

## MONTEZUMA'S WELL

Montezuma's Well, Arizona is a limestone sink more than 400 feet across. A natural lake at the bottom is about 55 feet deep and the water surface is about 70 feet below the rim of the sink. A natural spring replenishes the lake at a rate of approximately 1.5 million gallons per day much as it did during the Sinagua era.

The presence of so much water attracted Sinagua settlers who used it for domestic purposes and irrigated adjoining farm fields. Reminders of their presence include the remnants of two pueblos on the rim, three small cliff dwellings in the western ledges and several rooms hidden in a large cave at the base. Most were occupied from approximately 1125 through about 1400 A.D. The site also protects several hundred yards of "fossilized" irrigation canals frozen in place by lime precipitating from irrigation water.

The Well is located just east of Interstate Highway 17 along a well-signed side road. Exit the highway at Exit 293 near McGuireville and follow the signs north. There are no services at the site and it is closed on Christmas Day. It is open daily the rest of the year, from 8 a.m. to 5 p.m. (winter) or 6 p.m. (summer). There is no fee to visit the Well and there are no services at the site.

## MONUMENT VALLEY NAVAJO TRIBAL PARK

Monument Valley is a broad, flat bowl along Arizona's northern border. The land is speckled with red buttes and spectacular sandstone spires memorialized in classic John Ford westerns including Stagecoach, She Wore a Yellow Ribbon and Cheyenne Autumn.

Ancestral Puebloans from Kayenta settled parts of the region and exploited its natural resources. Their structures were not as imposing as many elsewhere and none have been developed for visitation. Today, most visitors are attracted by the majestic vistas, purple sage and opportunities to buy Native American Crafts from the current , Navajo residents.

Visitors enchanted by the scenery can drive for miles, but the Visitors' Center at the Navajo Tribal Park is the best place to start. Admission is $5 per person, children under 10 are free and the Park is open from 6 a.m. to 8 p.m. during the summer. Winter opening

*Ruins on Cedar Mesa near Mule Canyon. Photo by Eric Skopec*

is delayed until 8 a.m. The park is closed Christmas day and Thanksgiving afternoon. A scenic driving tour at the Center displays many of the varied landscape features and a four wheel drive vehicle is recommended. The Park is located along the Arizona-Utah border and the well-signed Visitors' Center is one mile east of U.S. highway 163. No lodging is available in the park, but services are available in Kayenta, Arizona, 22 miles south.

## 👋 👋 MULE CANYON AND CAVE TOWERS RUINS

Mule Canyon, about 20 miles southwest of Blanding, Utah, was an overflow area for the Ancestral Puebloans. They occupied the canyon for a short time around 750 A.D. and returned for a century and a half beginning around 1000 A.D. Most recognizable structures date from the second occupation and archeological evidence indicates that the population peaked around 1150 A.D., shortly before the people withdrew from the area.

Roadside Ruin is the most accessible site in Mule Canyon. Excavated and stabilized, Roadside Ruin consists of a twelve-room pueblo, kiva and tower. An easy, wheelchair accessible trail leads from the parking area to the site and interpretive signs facilitate self-guided tours. A slightly longer walk leads to Cave Tower Ruins on the plateau overlooking Mule Canyon. Do not attempt to descend into the Canyon from this point!

Remote ruins in Mule Canyon require more demanding hikes, but offer "more authentic" experiences. From a separate trailhead, an unsigned but well-worn trail leads into the Canyon. The first ruin is approximately 1 1/4 miles from the trailhead and sites are spaced about a half mile apart for the next four miles. Some are high on the cliff face and climbing to them is discouraged. Binoculars and long camera lenses are safer ways to see them.

The Roadside Ruin parking area is adjacent to Highway 95, 19 miles west of its intersection with Highway 191. At the sign, turn north on County Road SJ 263 and drive to the parking area. The trailhead for the remote ruins is a half mile east of the Roadside Ruin area on a dirt road near mile marker 102 south of highway 95. High clearance vehicles are required beyond the first gate and people driving sedans are advised to park outside the gate and walk the half mile to the trailhead.

Both trailheads are open year round and services are limited to vault toilets. There is no admission fee, but those hiking to the remote ruins will need to complete a back country permit at the trailhead kiosk.

### MUSEUM OF INDIAN ARTS AND CULTURE

The Museum of Indian Arts and Culture in Santa Fe, New Mexico houses an outstanding collection of Native American artifacts. Highlights include a 151-foot-long hunting net made of human hair, a ceremonial bead cache from Chaco Canyon and some early Navajo textiles as well as a large collection of Navajo blankets from the 19th century. The Museum also serves as a repository for artifacts recovered on federal, state and tribal lands.

The Museum regularly hosts events celebrating the Native American heritage. Prominent authors describe their work and sign copies, Native American groups present dances and stories and artists demonstrate their work. The schedule of events is posted online at http://www.miaclab.org/events.

The Museum is at 710-708 Camino Lejo just off Old Santa Fe Trail adjacent to the Museum of Spanish Colonial Art, Wheelwright Museum of the American Indian and the Museum of International Folk Art. The Museum is open from 10 a.m. to 5 p.m. Tuesday through Sunday year round. Admission is $6 for New Mexico residents, $8 for nonresidents and children 16 and under are free. Free tours by the museum's docents are offered on a convenient schedule.

### MUSEUM OF NORTHERN ARIZONA

The Museum of Northern Arizona in Flagstaff, Arizona is a private, not for profit institution founded in 1928 as a repository for Native American artifacts recovered on the Colorado Plateau. It has an outstanding collection of Ancestral Puebloan artifacts including sandals, stone points and pottery. Researchers at the Museum work with the Hopi Cultural Preservation Office to explore expressions of Hopi values and lifeways in pottery, murals, basketry and petroglyphs.

"Native Peoples of the Colorado Plateau" is a permanent exhibit documenting 12,000 years of settlement in the region. Other current exhibits include a Hopi mural displaying their oral history and prehistoric ceramics the Hopi regard as footsteps of their ancestors.

The Museum is located at 3101 N. Fort Valley Rd., 3 miles north of downtown Flagstaff, Arizona on US Highway 180. It is open from 9 a.m. to 5 p.m. daily except Thanksgiving, Christmas and New Year's Day. Regular admission is $7 with discounts for seniors, students, Native Americans and children.

*A small panel of pertroglyphs from the Nampaweap Petroglyph Site. Photo by Chris Skopec*

## NAMPAWEAP PETROGLYPH SITE

The Nampaweap Petroglyph Site is one of the largest collections of glyphs on the Arizona Strip north of the Grand Canyon. The glyphs are concentrated along a half-mile stretch on the wall of a shallow, but well watered cleft in the side of Mount Trumbull. Most of the glyphs were carved by Ancestral Puebloans, but Archaic and Paiute glyphs are present as well. Images include human figures, bighorn sheep, snakes and lizards as well as circles, spirals and lines.

No permanent structures have been found near the glyph panels and Native Americans probably lived in temporary shelters while hunting and gathering in the area. Remnants of several villages are present at Pipe Spring National Monument about 45 miles away and their residents may have created much of the rock art.

Visits require walking along well worn dirt tracks, through knee-high grasses and between low lying shrubs. There are rattlesnakes in the area and you should exercise appropriate caution.

There are no services at the site and admission is free. From St. George, Utah drive Quail Hill Road (BLM Road 1069) to Main Street Valley Road (County Road 5), drive

*Owachomo Bridge, Natural Bridges National Monument. Photo courtesy of the National Parks Service*

past Mt. Trumbull to the Arkansas Ranch Road (BLM 1028), turn right and drive south about 1 mile to the signed parking area. Alternately, visit Pipe Spring National Monument and ask for directions. Both routes require driving on graded dirt roads and a high clearance four-wheel drive vehicle may be needed following precipitation.

## NATURAL BRIDGES NATIONAL MONUMENT

Natural Bridges National Monument, near Blanding, Utah, was home to a thriving Ancestral Puebloan population. From about 700 through 1270 A.D., people from the Kayenta region settled here and were followed by Mesa Verde settlers around 1200 A.D. Both groups followed earlier occupations by Archaic people and archeologists believe population levels varied with weather conditions, increasing during moister cycles and dissipating during drier periods.

Today, Natural Bridges National Monument is most noted for its scenic beauty. Auto touring, camping and hiking are the principal attractions. The Horsecollar Ruin with a largely intact kiva and eight to ten rooms is the best known archeological site. Smaller structures and petroglyphs are scattered throughout the Monument. Some can be viewed from overlooks while others can be visited on short hikes.

Natural Bridges is at the end of Highway 275 off Highway 95 about 35 miles west of Blanding. The Monument is open year round and the Visitor Center is open daily from 9:00 a.m. to 5:30 p.m. except Thanksgiving Day, December 25th and January 1st. The admission fee is $6 for vehicles. Campsites are available in a small campground on a first-come, first-served basis. Few other services are available in Natural Bridges National Monument but gas, food and lodging are plentiful in nearby towns such as Blanding, Monticello and Cortez, Colorado.

## NAVAJO NATIONAL MONUMENT

Navajo National Monument preserves a portion of the Ancestral Puebloan homeland centered on Tsegi Canyon in Arizona. The Canyon is a dramatic gash in a high mesa, and numerous side canyons slice into the surrounding landform. The fall colors are spectacular in the late afternoon, especially after the occasional thundershower.

Named for the modern town of Kayenta, the Ancestral Puebloans here developed a distinct cultural pattern that rivaled those of Mesa Verde and Chaco Canyon. From this rugged but sheltering environment, the Ancestral Puebloans reached out to occupy large segments of Black Mesa, settled parts of Canyon de Chelly, and seeded populations along the Virgin River in Nevada, Monument Valley and around the Grand Canyon.

There are good views from the park headquarters, but only two sites are open to visitors: Betatakin and Keet Seel. Both require substantial hikes with advance reservations and should be attempted only by hikers in good physical condition. Call ahead for reservations: (928) 672-2700.

Navajo National Monument is in northeast Arizona near the junction of US Highway 160 and State Road 562. The Monument Headquarters is open daily from 8 a.m. to 5 p.m. and until 7 p.m. during the summer. There is a modest entrance fee, but camping is free at two campgrounds with 45 sites. Guest services at the Monument are limited, but there is a general store at the highway intersection and a pleasant café at Tsegi, eleven miles northeast of the junction. You will also find the nearest lodging in Tsegi, but there is greater selection of services in Kayenta, 19 miles from the junction.

## NEWSPAPER ROCK

Newspaper Rock is a large sandstone boulder in eastern Utah. Named for a 200 square foot area with a high concentration of petroglyphs, the Rock is one of the most accessible collections of carved glyphs in the southwest.

For nearly 2,000 years, Native Americans carved figures on Newspaper Rock. Recognizable glyphs include animals and human figures as well as handprints and footprints. There are also abstract and geometric forms and a few unrecognizable symbols. Many cultures have contributed to the panel and large groups are attributed to the Ancestral Puebloans, Fremont and Navajo.

Today, Newspaper Rock is protected as a State Historical Monument just a few miles off Utah 211 between Moab and Monticello, Utah. The turn off is well signed. The site is open year round and there is no admission fee. Services at the site are limited to parking, picnic areas, and restrooms. Motels and other services are available in proximate communities including Monticello, Blanding and Moab. Coincidentally, there is another "Newspaper Rock" in Petrified Forest National Monument and both are worth seeing.

## ❧❧❧ NINE MILE CANYON

Utah's Nine Mile Canyon was home to Archaic and Fremont peoples as well as Utes and Anglo settlers in subsequent eras. All left tangible reminders of their presence, but greatest interest now attaches to the rock art. The Canyon is often called the world's longest art gallery.

The Canyon was named by John Wesley Powell who noted its location 9 miles from another waypoint. The Canyon is actually over 40 miles long and a small stream provides year round water as in ancient times. The Fremont occupied the area for three centuries, roughly 950 to 1250 A.D. They left hundreds of pit houses, granaries and rock shelters as well as miles of irrigation ditches and rock art panels. More than a thousand panels and 10,000 glyphs have been noted and surveys are far from complete. Three smaller canyons intersect Nine Mile Canyon and rock art is often clustered near their junctions.

Today, archeological sites in the Canyon are threatened by the Bureau of Land Management's proposal to lease large tracts for gas drilling. For now, the proposal is "on hold" but the threat remains very real and citizens groups have united to oppose it. They note that remediation efforts cannot protect undiscovered sites and rock art panels. You can follow current developments on our companion Web site, www.Anasazi Adventure.com

Nine Mile Canyon is located in eastern Utah off Road 2200 East (Soldier Creek Road) from Highway 6/191. Visiting sites in the Canyon entails driving the graded dirt road along its length stopping frequently to visit sites and hike along the base of canyon walls. Published "what to see" guides are available, but exploring on your own may be more rewarding. As you venture into the Canyon, please respect the rights of private land owners and beware of heavy truck traffic. In addition, this is a wilderness area in which few services are available. Helpful Bureau of Land Management information is available at http://www.blm.gov/ut/st/en/fo/price/recreation/9mile.html

## ❧ NOGALES CLIFF HOUSE

The Nogales Cliff House near Cuba, New Mexico is a remnant of an Ancestral Puebloan village. Built by members of the Gallina culture around 1000 A.D., the village was occupied for just over a century.

Today only the upper section of the pueblo is visible and the lower section has eroded away. Archaeologists believe the pueblo originally had about 30 living and storage rooms on two levels.

The site is about a mile from the parking area. Most of the hike is along an easy, shaded path but the final 300 feet are very steep with multiple switchbacks.

The Nogales Cliff House is roughly 30 miles south of Cuba, New Mexico. Much of the route is paved but the final few miles are graded dirt that require a high clearance, four-wheel drive vehicle. Portions may be impassible following heavy rain or snow. You should, inquire locally in Cuba, New Mexico. The now closed Cuba Visitors Bureau still has directions on their Web site at www.cubanm.org/index.html.

## 🖐🖐 OHKAY OWINGEH

With a population of nearly 7,000, Ohkay Owingeh is one of New Mexico's largest Tewa-speaking pueblos. Named Pueblo de San Juan de los Caballeros by the Spanish, Ohkay Owingeh is recovering its cultural traditions and in 2005 reverted to its ancestral name. Coincidentally, you will still see San Juan Pueblo on older maps and in US Postal Service guides, but residents may be offended if you use the Spanish name.

Around 1200 A.D., ancestors of the Ohkay Owingeh people immigrated to the area from southern Colorado. They established villages on both sides of the Rio Grande, but Yungé Owingeh on the west side of the river was remodeled by Spanish colonists and subsequently abandoned. In contrast, Ohkay Owingeh has been occupied on its current site for about 800 years.

Today, the pueblo is the headquarters of the Eight Northern Indian Pueblos Council and home to a flourishing craft tradition. Village life is orchestrated by traditional structures dividing the population into Winter and Summer People each of which is responsible for conducting specific ceremonies. There are Buffalo Dances, Basket Dances and a Cloud Dance at various times of the year and the Deer Dance is performed in January or February.

Ohkay Owingeh is about a half dozen miles north of Espanola, New Mexico just off State Road 68. The village is open year round and can arrange tours, dances and representative native foods for groups with advance notice.

## DNA OLD PUEBLO ARCHEOLOGY CENTER

The Old Pueblo Archeology Center in Tucson, Arizona is a not for profit organization dedicated to educating children and adults alike. The Center conducts "Discovery Tours" of the Hopi mesas, Zuni Pueblo, Canyon de Chelly, Casa Grande Ruins, Chaco Canyon and other archeological sites as well as rock art clusters. Fees vary and you can find the Center's schedule online at http://www.oldpueblo.org/index.html For information about particular tours, email info@oldpueblo.org or call (520) 798-1201.

## 🖐 ORABI

Sometimes called "Old Orabi" or "Oravi", Orabi is one of the oldest continuously occupied villages in the United States. The village dates to the early 11th century but is surrounded by sites almost 400 years older. Please see the Hopi Mesas entry for additional details.

## 🖐 PAINTED HAND PUEBLO

Painted Hand Pueblo is an unexcavated partially stabilized Ancestral Puebloan site northwest of Cortez, Colorado. Most of the Pueblo III structures against the cliff face have collapsed and a partially stabilized tower atop a boulder is the site's focal point.

Painted Hand Pueblo is located in a remote section of Canyon of the Ancients National Monument. Reaching it entails driving over graded dirt roads and a high clearance vehicle is recommended. Four-wheel drive is helpful following snow or rain.

From the small graded parking area, a short trail follows the cliff edge and drops down to circle the site. The hike is easy and includes several overlooks. Healthy doses of insect repellent will make the walk more enjoyable in summer months. First time visitors should

*Painted Hand Pueblo, Canyon of the Ancients National Monument. Photo by Eric Skopec*

begin at the Anasazi Heritage Center where maps and information about current road conditions are available.

Please see the Anasazi Heritage Center entry for directions and additional information.

## 👐 PAINTED ROCKS PETROGLYPH SITE

Approximately 90 miles southwest of Phoenix, Arizona, the Painted Rocks Petroglyph Site provides easy access to rock mounds and boulders etched with petroglyphs. The earliest glyphs date to the close of the Paleo-Indian period (9500 to 6000 B.C.), but most are from the Hohokam era (200-1400 A.D.). Most glyphs depict animals, people and geometric shapes while some commemorate historic events.

The site features an easy half-mile trail around and through the greatest concentration of glyphs. Interpretive plaques explain the area's geologic history and the cultural affiliations of some glyphs. Visitors are cautioned to stay on the trail, both to protect the glyphs and to avoid rattlesnakes. Visitation is light, especially during the summer months when temperatures can reach 120F. Winter (October through April) visits are more appealing but the temperatures can still reach into the 80s.

Exit Interstate Highway 8 at Painted Rocks Dam Road (Exit 102) approximately 12.5 miles west of Gila Bend and turn north on the paved Painted Rocks Dam Road. After just

71

over ten miles, turn onto the unpaved Rocky Point Road and watch for the sign identifying the site. Facilities include picnic tables, barbeque grills, steel fire rings and a vault toilet but no water is available.

Coincidentally, Painted Rocks was a state park until 1989 and some maps still list it as Painted Rocks State Park.

## PALATKI HERITAGE SITE

The Palatki Heritage Site preserves a picturesque cliff dwelling and rock art site southwest of Sedona, Arizona. Built and occupied by the Sinagua around 1130 A.D., Palatki was abandoned by 1300. Originally, the cliff dwelling stood two or more stories tall but several upper story rooms have collapsed into the rooms below and rubble trails down the cliff face in front of the dwelling. Estimating population is difficult, but Palatki was probably one of the larger villages in the immediate area.

A converted farmhouse serves as a Visitors' Center. Restrooms and water are available and there is a small bookstore. Two well-marked trails lead to the cliff face. One directs visitors to the dwelling while the other leads to a rock art site. Neither trail is particularly difficult, but both require modest amounts of climbing that may be difficult for people with knee or respiratory problems.

The site is open daily from 9:30 a.m. to 3:30 p.m., but is closed on Thanksgiving and Christmas day. It also closes when weather conditions render the graded dirt roads impassible. Reservations and a Red Rock Pass are required. Occasionally, you may be able to make reservations for the same day, but its best to call two or three days ahead of your planned visit: (928) 282-3854. During dry weather, the road is passable in a passenger car but conditions may change rapidly. Inquire about directions, reservations and road conditions when you purchase your Red Rock Pass.

## PARK OF THE CANALS

Park of The Canals in Mesa, Arizona is a lightly used 30-acre preserve. It contains 4,500 feet of Hohokam irrigation canals some of which were reused by anglo settlers in the late 1800s. The park also contains an extensive desert botanical garden with about 150 species of cacti and other vegetation.

Recent reports indicate that the Park is in some disrepair. Vandalism and crime have become problematic and you should exercise caution when visiting. The Arizona Museum of Natural History is a pleasant and informative alternative. The Park is located at 710 N. Horne and is open from sunrise to 10 p.m. There is no admission charge and you can visit the Park's web site for updates http://www.parkofthecanals.org.

## PAROWAN GAP

Parowan Gap is a 600-foot deep cleft in the Red Hills of south central Utah. It is a natural east-west passage through the hills and travelers have used the route for at least 8,000 years. More than 50 archeological sites have been recorded in the immediate area along with nearly a hundred petroglyph panels containing more than 1,500 figures. Glyphs are concentrated on smooth boulders at the east end of the gap and include snakes, lizards, mountain sheep, human figures and bear claws as well as geometric designs. Researchers

*Pecos Pueblo, Pecos National Histrorical Park. Photo courtesy of the National Park Service.*

comparing the glyphs to topographic features have concluded that several are maps while two Spanish crosses mark the passage of 17th century explorers.

The glyphs are a National Historic Landmark and recent research has focused on stone cairns on the level plain east of the Gap. Visually, the Gap is a deeply carved V that channels light from the setting sun. As the relative positions of the sun and earth change over the course of a year, the last light of the day falls on different cairns. Native Americans may have used the Gap as a massive solar observatory and calendar. Positions of other celestial bodies may have been monitored as well and research is an ongoing activity.

Parowan Gap is just a few miles off Interstate 15. Follow Exit 62 to Utah 130 north for 13 miles and turn east after 2.5 miles onto a gravel road passing through the gap. Off road parking is readily available but there are no services or admission fee.

### 🖐🖐🖐 PECOS NATIONAL HISTORICAL PARK

Abandoned structures at Pecos National Historical Park near Santa Fe, New Mexico document more than 1,100 years of southwestern life and record pivotal events in the evolution of Puebloan society. Archaic people may have frequented the area, but 9th century pit houses are the earliest known structures. Pueblos appear early in the 12th century. Shortly after 1300 A.D., residents abandoned small villages in the area and the population aggregated in large structures including Pecos Pueblo. By the middle of the 15th century, the pueblo had grown into a five story fortress-like structure surrounded by a perimeter wall with a population of 2,000 people.

The Puebloans welcomed Spanish explorers in the 16th century, expelled them in the 1680 Pueblo Revolt, and welcomed them back in 1693. Early 19th century epidemics nearly wiped out the population and in 1838 the survivors abandoned the site and joined their relatives at Jemez Pueblo.

Today, a 1 1/4 mile interpretive trail leads from the Visitors' Center through the heart of the abandoned pueblo. Designated stops include the Spanish Mission destroyed in 1680 and the site of a mission built after the Spanish returned. During the summer, guided tours are conducted at 10 a.m. daily and guided tours of proximate ruins are offered on Wednesday and Friday afternoons.

Pecos National Historical Park is 25 miles east of Santa Fe adjacent to Interstate 25. Appropriate exits are well-signed and the Visitors' Center is open from 8 a.m. to 6 p.m. during the summer. Winter hours are 8 a.m. to 4:30 p.m. and the Park is closed on Christmas and New Years day. Admission is $3 per adult and services are available in nearby Pecos Village as well as Santa Fe.

### ꙮꙮ PETRIFIED FOREST NATIONAL PARK

Petrified Forest National Park straddles Interstate Highway 40 near the center of Arizona. The Puerco River was the dominant feature during Ancestral Puebloan times and scatters of petrified wood are found throughout the Park. Today it protects over 218,000 acres with three major archeological sites listed on the National Register of Historic Places.

Puerco Ruin with at least 125 rooms surrounding a central plaza is the largest ruin in the park. It is situated near a large concentration of petrified wood that was quarried throughout antiquity. The structure was occupied around 1250 A.D. and abandoned near the end of the 14th century.

Newspaper Rock, a large sandstone boulder covered with petroglyphs, is the best-known site in the park. Geometric designs, quadrupeds, footprints and handprints predominate, but you will also see other creatures and line drawings. Smaller boulders in the vicinity also served as artists' tablets and it is easy to lose track of time while viewing and photographing the glyphs.

Finally, Agate House is the most colorful site in the park. It is an eight-room pueblo made entirely of petrified wood and was probably occupied between 900 and 1200 A.D. Hearths found in two rooms indicate that the structure was occupied on a year round basis.

The park is open year round except Christmas day. Hours vary with the season, and typically run from 9 a.m. to 5 p.m. with longer hours during peak season. There are no camping or lodging facilities in the Park, but services are readily available along Interstate 40 and in the proximate communities including Joseph City, Holbrook and Navajo. There is a modest entrance fee. Most visitors exit Interstate 40 to follow U.S. Highway 180 south to the park's south entrance and drive north through the park to return to Interstate 40.

Coincidentally, there is a State Historical Monument named "Newspaper Rock" in Utah. Both are worth seeing.

*Ancestral Puebloan petroglyphs. Photo courtesy of www.riparian.smugmug.com*

## 🖐🖐🖐 PETROGLYPH NATIONAL MONUMENT

Located adjacent to Albuquerque, New Mexico, Petroglyph National Monument was created in 1990 to protect an estimated 25,000 petroglyphs.

The park straddles a gigantic rift separating the Colorado Plateau from the Great Plains and features a 17-mile long escarpment of fractured basalt. A fine patina of desert varnish coats exposed cliffs and tumbled boulders making them ideal canvases for rock art. Artists have worked these surfaces for several millennia and the oldest images may be over 3,000 years old. The Ancestral Puebloans, their descendents, Spanish colonists and nineteenth-century settlers all carved glyphs.

There are petroglyphs in all three units of the Monument. The Visitors' Center and the Piedras Marcadas Pueblo along with Ancestral Puebloan, Christian and cowboy glyphs are in the Rinconada Canyon unit. The Boca Negra unit features three paved trails with interpretive signs and a fourth, unpaved trail for a less structured experience. The third unit, Piedras Marcadas, also has many petroglyphs as well as cinder cones, lava tubes and other lava forms.

Your visit should start at the Visitor's Center, 3.5 miles north of Interstate 40 at the intersection of Unser and Western Trail. The Monument is open from 8 a.m. to 5p.m. year round except for Thanksgiving, Christmas, and New Years. There is no admission fee, but the City of Albuquerque charges for parking at the Boca Negra Unit. Few services are available in the Monument, but food and lodging are readily available at restaurants, grocery stores, motels and campsites in the surrounding area.

## ᴡᴡ PICURIS PUEBLO

Of the nineteen surviving pueblos, Picuris Pueblo near Santa Fe, New Mexico suffered most at the hands of the Spanish. Residents were blamed for the Pueblo Revolt and returning Spanish imposed oppressive taxes and deliberately introduced smallpox. The precontact population estimated at 5,000 was reduced to fewer than 300 people who abandoned the area for a time. Around 1706, a handful of survivors returned and began rebuilding their community.

Today, the Pueblo offers a variety of recreational activities. Visitors can fish, hike, eat traditional foods and shop for authentic crafts. In addition, tours of archeological sites are available. Self-guided tours require permits sold at the Visitors' Center along with still photography permits. With advance reservations, you can also take a 3-hour guided walking tour of archeological sites, churches and the museum or a vehicle tour visiting agricultural terraces, cisterns, irrigation systems and flood control features.

There is no fee for entering the Pueblo and tour fees vary with the number of people. Shorter walking tours average about $5 per person while longer tours are proportionately more expensive. I recommend you establish prices when you call ahead for reservations: (505) 587-2519

Picuris is about 25 miles north of Santa Fe. Drive New Mexico 84 north to Espanola, turn north on New Mexico 68 to the town of Dixon and east on New Mexico 75. Watch for the signed exit.

## ᴡᴡ PIPE SPRING NATIONAL MONUMENT

Pipe Spring is one of our less-visited national monuments. Located on the bit of Arizona between the Grand Canyon and the Utah border, the monument consists of 40 acres surrounded by the Kaibab Indian Reservation.

During the late nineteenth and early twentieth centuries, the monument was the core of an extensive cattle ranch that spread over the adjoining lands. As many as 5,000 long horn cattle once grazed on the arid plateau. Today, interpretation at the Monument focuses on Mormon occupancy which began in the 1860s. Guided tours lead visitors through a large fortified house known as Windsor Castle and related stone houses are open for self-guided tours.

The area has a much longer history and people have used the natural spring water for more than 12,000 years. Roughly three quarters of the Monument bears evidence of Ancestral Puebloan occupation and there are several sites of interest. The half-mile-loop Ridge Trail behind the Castle walks visitors past a few glyphs and through an unexcavated Basketmaker village. There is a large unexcavated great kiva near the Monument's administrative headquarters and knowledgeable interpreters can also point out the location of buried pueblos within the Monument's grounds. Staff can also provide directions to the Nampaweap Petroglyph Site and northern rim of the Grand Canyon.

Pipe Spring National Monument is located on Arizona State Route 389 approximately 15 miles west of Fredonia. Admission is $5.00 per person and children under 16 are

*Windsor Castle at Pipe Spring National Monument. Photo by Eric Skopec*

admitted free. The Visitors' Center is open from 7 a.m. to 5 p.m. during the summer and opens an hour later during the winter. There are few services at the monument but a convenience store on 389 has a variety of foods and there is a RV park near the Monument's headquarters.

## POJOAQUE PUEBLO

Pojoaque Pueblo near Santa Fe, New Mexico occupies a bit of land first settled around 500 A.D. The area's population peaked in the late 15th century, but subsequent years have not been kind to the people. They abandoned the pueblo after the Pueblo Revolt of 1680 but a few families were induced to return and the pueblo was refounded in 1706. Smallpox, drought and encroachment devastated the population and the pueblo was again abandoned around 1913. In 1934 the Commissioner of Indian Affairs convinced a few families to return and the modern pueblo dates to that time.

With its turbulent past, there are no archeological sites of note open to casual visitors. However, the people have worked to recover their traditions and founded the Poeh Cultural Center in 1988. Dedicated to preserving traditions of the Tewa-speaking pueblos, the Center exhibits pueblo art and hosts traditional dances on weekends. A museum followed in 1991 and its permanent collection includes paintings, jewelry, pottery and textiles as well as an estimated 10,000 photographs ranging from early Edward S. Curtis prints to snapshots of contemporary Pueblo life.

The Pueblo is 15 miles north of Santa Fe on highway 84/285 and the exit is signed. There is no fee to enter the Pueblo or Museum but donations are appreciated. Services are available in Santa Fe and at many points along the route to Pojoaque.

### POSHUOUINGA RUINS

Poshuouinga Ruins are the remains of a large Ancestral Puebloan village dating to the 14th century. Situated in the Chama River Valley, Poshuouinga Ruins is along side US highway 84 about 2.5 miles south of Abiquiu, New Mexico.

Today, a well marked trail leads from the parking area up to a terrace from which you can view the site. Visible remains include outlines of a pueblo with 700 ground floor rooms, two plazas and a large kiva. The top of the rise offers better views and signage includes an artist's reconstruction of the pueblo.

There are no services at the site and no admission fee.

### PUEBLITOS OF THE DINETAH

About two centuries after the Ancestral Puebloans abandoned the four corners area, small groups of nomadic people from the north reoccupied much of their former territory. In the next few decades, the people developed a unique culture that we call Navajo and their name for the reoccupied territory is Dinetah, or "homeland."

Near the end of the 17th century, the Navajo began building defensive structures called pueblitos. Made of unshaped sandstone blocks and mud mortar, pueblitos are typically built on rock outcroppings or cliff edges. They generally have 6 to 8 rooms and may have towers. Rock art is frequently found nearby.

There is a large concentration of pueblitos in Largo Canyon east of Farmington, New Mexico. Most date from the end of the 17th century and many are remarkably well preserved.

Visits are possible year round, but road and weather conditions are highly variable. Spring and fall are attractive times, but thunderstorms can turn the road to mush. High clearance four-wheel drive vehicles are recommended and many people prefer to travel with professional guides. The San Juan County Archaeological Research Center at Salmon Ruins in Bloomfield, New Mexico conducts tours and you may ask for Larry Baker, (505) 632-2013. If you prefer to go on your own, begin at the Bureau of Land Management office in Farmington to pick up necessary maps and inquire about local conditions.

### PUEBLO BONITO

Pueblo Bonito is the largest and best-known Ancestral Puebloan great house. Built over even older pit houses, Bonito was expanded and remodeled many times and occupied from around 860 A.D. through the early 13th century. At it peak, it stood at least four stories tall and had over 800 rooms and 30 kivas.

Today, the structure has been stabilized and an interpretative trail leads visitors through and around it. One part of the trail requires bending and stooping, but visitors

*Pueblo Bonito, in Chaco Culture National Historic Park, at sunrise. Photo by Eric Skopec*

with limited mobility can easily walk around that section. During summer months, Park Service personnel conduct guided tours and a trail guide is available for those who prefer to visit on their own. A more detailed tour guide for Pueblo Bonito is available online at www.AnasaziAdventure.com.

Pueblo Bonito is one of the structures on the main loop at Chaco Culture National Historic Park. Please see the Park entry for directions and additional information.

## PUEBLO GRANDE DE NEVADA

Pueblo Grande de Nevada is Nevada's "lost city" and consists of villages inundated by Lake Mead. The villages are listed on the National Register of Historic Places and excavations produced evidence of human occupation as early as 8000 B.C.

Today the villages are long gone, but the Lost City Museum of Archeology in Overton, Nevada houses artifacts recovered during salvage excavations. Please see the Museum entry for directions and other information.

## PUEBLO GRANDE MUSEUM AND ARCHAEOLOGICAL PARK

Pueblo Grande Museum and Archaeological Park in Phoenix, Arizona preserves a 102 acre segment of a 14$^{th}$ century Hohokam village. Features of particular interest include a platform mound, excavated ball court, large irrigation canals and reproduced Hohokam dwellings. The Museum serves as a Visitors Center, displays artifacts from excavations and hosts permanent exhibitions about Hohokam agriculture, canal building, crafts and trade as well as workshops and hands on activities for children. Guided tours of the museum and park are available with advance reservations. Call for more information and reservations, (602) 495-0901.

The Museum and Archeological Park are located at 4619 E. Washington Street, the southeast corner of 44th Street and Washington in Phoenix. Admission is $5 for adults with discounts for seniors and children. Free parking is available and the Museum is open Monday through Saturday from 9 a.m. to 4:45 p.m. and Sunday from 1 p.m. to 4:45 p.m. From May through September, the Museum is closed on Sunday and Monday.

## ᘤ PUEBLO LA PLATA

Pueblo la Plata (Silver Creek Pueblo) is the most accessible site in the Agua Fria National Monument. Occupied between 1250 and 1450 A.D., the pueblo had between 80 and 100 rooms and was probably home to about 50 people. It was the central village in a cluster of hamlets built by little-known people of the Perry Mesa Tradition. They are believed to have migrated into the area from Hohokam regions to the south and their descendents may include the Yavapai Indians, but cultural relationships remain uncertain.

Today, visitors see the outlines of square rooms and standing walls that occasionally reach 6 feet in height. There are also quantities of broken pottery and substantial rock art panels are an easy walk from the Pueblo. Visitors are encouraged to explore cautiously because rattlesnakes are active much of the year.

Conditions in Agua Fria and at the Pueblo are primitive, and reaching the site requires an 8.3 mile drive over an unmarked dirt track. High clearance, 4 wheel drive vehicles are strongly recommended and visitors are advised to walk the last half mile to the site. Bureau of Land Management maps to the Pueblo are available at the entry kiosk and directions to the Monument are included in the Agua Fria National Monument entry.

## ᘤ ᘤ PUEBLO PINTADO

Pueblo Pintado is a large Chacoan great house in a detached unit of Chaco Culture National Historical Park. The pueblo is surrounded by the remains of at least 30 small houses and the unit protects a total of 160 acres.

Pueblo Pintado is an L-shaped great house built on a low ridge. It is smaller than many other Chacoan great houses, but it originally stood three stories tall with about 135 rooms. It also appears that a room block was added to the central plaza after initial construction. The site has not been excavated and a scattering of tree ring dates indicates that construction began around 1060 A.D. and continued for 30 or 40 years. In addition to the structure, visitors can see a relatively well-preserved Chacoan Road at the site. Beginning near the southwestern corner of the structure, the road runs west toward the head of Chaco Canyon and is most visible in early mornings and late afternoons when angular light highlights its features. Pueblo Pintado is approximately 15 miles south of the Chaco Culture National Historical Park.

There are no services at the site and dirt roads leading to it are unsigned. Staff at the Chaco Culture Visitors' Center can provide a map and information about current road conditions. Please see the Chaco Culture entry for directions and additional information.

*Pueblo Pintado. Photo by Eric Skopec*

## PUERCO RUIN

Puerco Ruin is the remnant of the largest Ancestral Puebloan structure in Petrified Forest National Park. Occupied for over a century, roughly 1250 to 1380 A.D., Puerco Ruin had about 76 rooms in two stories around a central plaza. It was probably home to about 75 people.

Puerco Ruin has been partially excavated and stabilized. A short interpretive trail circles the structure, but only a handful of rooms are intact. There are abundant petroglyphs nearby and images include human faces, bighorn sheep, antelope, birds, lizards and snakes.

See the Petrified Forest National Park entry for directions and other information.

## PUYE CLIFF DWELLINGS

The Puye Cliff Dwellings were the ancestral home of the Santa Clara Pueblo people. Located just a few miles east of the historic pueblo, the Puye' Cliff Dwellings were occupied for a little over 300 years, roughly 1250 to 1580 A.D.

The Cliff Dwellings were the heart of a large village consisting of both the rooms carved into the soft volcanic stone along the cliff face and a mesa-top pueblo. Excavated

81

in 1907, the pueblo had at least 740 rooms in 3 or 4 stories and its population may have reached 2,000 people. Carved stairs linked the pueblo with the cliff face rooms and kivas in the talus slope at its base. Petroglyphs carved into the cliff face include concentric circles, spirals, animals, human figures, masks and a horned or plumed serpent.

The Puye Clif Dwellings have been a tourist attraction for over a century, but closed to visitors in 2000. Limited guided tours resumed in 2008 and drop-in access is available now. Depending on weather conditions, the site will be open 7 days a week from 9:30 a.m. to 3 p.m. with tour prices between $7 and $30. To confirm hours and tour availability visit http://www.puyecliffs.org/index.html or call (888) 320-5008. The Puye Cliffs Welcome Center is on N.M. 30 about 2 miles southwest of Española and the ruins are located about seven miles further west.

## ᗰᗰ QUARAI RUINS

Quarai Ruins are the best preserved of the three principal sites in Salinas Pueblo Missions National Monument. Built by the Spanish at the close of the 16th century, remnants of Nuestra Señora de La Purisima Concepcion de Cuarac still stand about 40 feet tall. Also visible are some remains of a pre-contact pueblo that stood on the site.

Quarai Ruins are 8 miles north of Mountainair, New Mexico just off State Highway 55. There is a Visitors' Center at the site along with a half-mile trail through the ruins. Please see the Salinas Pueblo Missions National Monument for additional information.

## ᗰ RANGE CREEK CANYON

In 2004, news media exposed what had been a closely guarded secret. Headlining "Canyon Holds Ancient Civilization Secrets," the Associated Press announced that extensive Fremont ruins in Range Creek Canyon were being surveyed by archeologists.

The land was owned by cattle rancher Waldo Wilcox who protected the sites and subsequently sold his property to the state of Utah. Visited briefly by archeologists in the 1920s, none of the sites were formally surveyed and researchers are now undertaking the first complete evaluation of the Fremont remnants. To date, they have recorded over 300 sites in just 5% of the Canyon system. Their finds include pit houses, petroglyphs and granaries, one of which was still a third full with parched wild grass seed and corn.

Located in east central Utah, access to Range Creek Canyon is controlled by the Utah Division of Wildlife Resources. Only 28 people per day are allowed to enter the Canyon and permits must be secured in advance. The Canyon is open annually from April 15th through December 1st depending on road and weather conditions. For information about permits and current conditions, please visit http://wildlife.utah.gov/range_creek/index.php

## RATTLESNAKE PUEBLO

Rattlesnake Pueblo is the stabilized remnant of an Ancestral Puebloan village occupied 1325 to 1390 A.D. Located near Springerville, Arizona the 90-room structure is generally rectangular with an enclosed plaza at one end and an enclosed square kiva at the other. It was home to about 15 families who farmed the now submerged flood plains along the Little Colorado River.

The Pueblo was excavated in the 1990s and some artifacts are displayed in the Lyman Lake Visitors' Center. Most of the structure was reburied after excavation, but four rooms are open for viewing.

Rattle Snake Pueblo is in Lyman Lake State Park and a short interpretive trail leads to the site. An informative trail guide is available and ranger-guided tours are conducted seasonally.

Lyman Lake State Park and Rattlesnake Pueblo are currently closed. Please see the main Park entry additional information.

## ❧ RATTLESNAKE RIDGE RUINS

Rattlesnake Ridge Ruins near Cuba, New Mexico are the remains of an Ancestral Puebloan village occupied between 1000 and 1200 A.D. Its residents were members of the Gallina Culture, a smaller less known group that was at least partially isolated from developments elsewhere in the southwest.

Today, a short moderately steep trail leads from the parking area to a standing tower and overlook. Remnants of other structures are scattered along nearly a mile of the ridge. Most are unexcavated and mounds are the most recognizable reminders of other structures.

Rattlesnake Ridge Ruins are roughly 35 miles west of Cuba, New Mexico. Much of the route is paved but portions may require high clearance, four-wheel drive vehicles and even they are likely to get stuck following heavy rain or snowfall. Inquire locally to check on current conditions and get directions. The now closed Cuba Visitors Bureau still has directions on their Web site at http://www.cubanm.org/index.html.

## RAVEN SITE

The Raven Site near St. Johns, Arizona is the remnant of an Ancestral Puebloan village overlooking the Little Colorado River. The White Mountain Archeological Center was created to preserve the site and charged fees to participate in excavations. Commercial operations were well publicized and you may still see references to the Raven Site, but the Center closed in the 1990s.

The Archeological Conservancy now owns the Raven Site and renamed it the Sherwood Ranch Pueblo in honor of Wendel and Ruth Sherwood who donated the land. The site is not open to the public, but occasionally the Conservancy hosts guided tours. Please see the Archaeological Conservancy entry for additional details.

## DNA RED ROCK PASS PROGRAM

The area surrounding Sedona, Arizona is famous for its stunning red sandstone cliffs and well-preserved archeological sites. Montezuma's Castle is the most famous, but Montezuma's Well, cliff dwellings at Hononki and Palatki and petroglyphs at the V Bar V site are all worth visiting.

To simplify visiting these sites and parking along scenic byways, the Forest Service created the Red Rock Pass Program. The pass provides admission to the archeological sites and entitles you to park in designated areas along the scenic routes. Daily passes cost $5 per car, weekly passes are $15 and both come with maps to the Heritage Sites and other features.

Passes may be purchased at the Red Rock Ranger District office, Sedona Oak Creek Chamber of Commerce, North Gateway Visitor Center, Peaks Ranger District office, Mormon Lake Ranger District office, Coconino Forest Supervisor's office, Verde Ranger District office and at commercial vendors including grocery stores as well as from self-service vending machines at most trailheads.

People with America the Beautiful passes as well as unexpired National Parks Passes, Golden Eagle, Golden Age, and Golden Access Passports are exempt from fees, but it is still a good idea to stop at one of the distribution centers to get a map, directions, and information about local conditions.

## ROMERO RUIN

Romero Ruin is a large Hohokam settlement near Tucson, Arizona. The archeological site covers 15 acres on a low ridge and includes remnants of pit houses, a walled village and a large ball court. The pit houses may have been built as early as 500 A.D. and the more visible structures were occupied between 1200 and 1500 A.D.

Today, Romero Ruin is part of Catalina State Park. Featured activities include hiking, bird watching, horseback riding and camping. There are eight hiking trails including the Romero Ruin Interpretive Trail. The Trail is an easy 3/4 mile hike that is especially well suited for children. A few Hohokam structures have been partially reconstructed, but most appear to be little more than rubble mounds. Fortunately, informative signs along the route point out important features.

Catalina State Park is 18 miles north of Tucson on Arizona Highway 77 (Oracle Road) and the exit is well-signed. The Park's Visitors' Center is open from 8 a.m. to 5 p.m. year round and the day use fee is $6 per vehicle. The nearest services are a mile away along the highway and 24 of the 48 campsites have water and electricity hookups for RVs. There are numerous motels and other services in Tucson.

## RUDD CREEK PUEBLO

Rudd Creek Pueblo is the popular name for the remains of an Ancestral Puebloan village near Springerville, Arizona. Occupied during the first half of the 13th century, the site was largely undisturbed until excavated by Arizona State University. Excavators exposed roughly 50 rooms and two kivas and recovered large quantities of artifacts.

Rudd Creek Pueblo sits on the edge of a large meadow adjacent to a small stream, Rudd Creek. Nearby basalt cliffs along the north side have many petroglyphs including images of snakes, lizards, footprints, men and a frog with splayed legs and toes.

Today, two easy trails lead from the visitors' center to the Pueblo. The one-mile High Point Loop Trail crosses Rudd Creek and climbs steeply to the petroglyphs. The view is spectacular and there are benches and interpretive signs along the trail. The Rudd Creek Loop Trail is an easy 3-mile loop along the banks of Rudd Creek and around the Pueblo where kiosks highlight features of the site.

Rudd Creek Pueblo and the surrounding 1,382 acres of forest, meadow and wetland form the Sipe White Mountain Wildlife Area managed by the State of Arizona. From Springerville, drive south on State routes 180/191 for approximately 2 miles and turn right onto the well maintained dirt road marked Sipe White Mountain Wildlife Area. The Area is open year round and a Visitors Center is open from 8 a.m. to 5 p.m. daily from May 15 to October 15.

## ꙮ SADDLEHORN HAMLET

Saddlehorn Hamlet is a small Pueblo III village along the Sand Canyon Trail. It was occupied for around three decades beginning in 1232. A well-preserved room and a standing wall in an alcove are the most visible features, but excavators also noted a kiva, two or three surface rooms and two towers on the cliff above. Many of these features have been reburied but the walls in the alcove have been stabilized and the site is a picturesque stopping point along the trail.

Saddlehorn Hamlet and the Sand Canyon Trail are located in Canyons of the Ancients National Monument. Please see the main entry for additional information.

## ꙮ ꙮ SALINAS PUEBLO MISSION NATIONAL MONUMENT

Salinas Pueblo Mission National Monument has three principal ruin sites that reflect the interaction of Native American and Spanish cultures. The area was first intensively settled around 1100 A.D. and overlapping Ancestral Puebloan and Mogollon influence produced the Native American cultural component. The Spanish colonized the area at the close of the 16th century and built mission churches at the site of existing pueblos during the 1620s.

Harsh Spanish rule aggravated cultural conflicts and Apache raids made pueblo life untenable. By the mid 1600s, Native American residents fled the area, probably moving to live with relatives in other pueblos. For their part, the Spanish were disappointed when the area did not produce appreciable wealth and abandoned the region following the Pueblo Revolt of 1680.

Located around Mountainair, New Mexico, the Monument is open daily except Thanksgiving, Christmas, and New Years day. Summer hours are 9 a.m. to 6 p.m. and the Monument closes an hour earlier during the winter. The Monument headquarters is located in Mountainair, New Mexico and there are separate Visitors' Centers at each of the principal ruins. Entries for Abo Ruins, Gran Quivira and Quarai Ruins provide directions and other information.

## ꙮ ꙮ SALMON RUINS AND HERITAGE PARK

Salmon Ruins is the remnant of a 250-room pueblo that once stood three or four stories tall. The tower kiva is well preserved and outlines of a great kiva are visible in the courtyard, but most standing walls are just over a single story tall.

Occupied from 1090 until 1280 A.D., Salmon Pueblo mirrors changes in the Ancestral Puebloan world. People from Chaco Canyon built the Pueblo and local people modified it as Chacoan influence waned. Many rooms were remodeled and changes in masonry style are evident in blocked in doorways and windows.

*The museum at Salmon Ruins and Heritage Park. Photo by Eric Skopec*

Salmon Pueblo is one of very few great houses excavated with modern methods and excavations produced a treasure trove of information . The Salmon family protected the site until the 1970s and Harvard educated Cynthia Irwin-Williams directed research. The museum at Salmon Ruins is one of the finest in the southwest.

Salmon Ruins and Heritage Park are located in Bloomfield, New Mexico. The San Juan County Museum Association manages the site and charges a modest entry fee. The site is open daily from 9 a.m. through 5 p.m. with reduced Sunday hours in the winter. Lodging and other services are available in Bloomfield and nearby communities including Aztec and Farmington.

## ✋ SAN FELIPE PUEBLO

San Felipe Pueblo near Bernalillo, New Mexico is among the most conservative pueblos. Outsiders are not encouraged to visit which explains the single handprint.

A few times a year, the pueblo welcomes outsiders. Local crafts, food and dances are well worth a visit if you happen to be in the area. The Feast Day of San Felipe on May 1 attracts hundreds of men, women and children dressed in traditional costumes to participate in the

Green Corn Dance. In addition, a traditional crafts show is held in October and you can call the tribal office to confirm the dates; (505) 867-3381.

San Felipe Pueblo is accessible from Interstate 25 ten miles north of Bernalillo. Leave the Interstate at exit 252 and follow the signed local road north for two miles. The tribe also operates a gas station, restaurant and gift shop as well as a modern casino.

## SAN ILDEFONSO PUEBLO

San Ildefonso Pueblo near Los Alamos, New Mexico has been the center of the pueblo arts revival and is noted for the black-on-black ware produced by its resident potters. The Pueblo was founded around 1300 A.D. by immigrants from the Mesa Verde region and their descendents have a strong sense of identity. They preserve ancient ceremonies and rituals, and conduct traditional dances a few of which are open to the public.

Highlights of a visit to San Ildefonso Pueblo include the San Ildefonso Mission Church built in 1711, San Ildefonso Pueblo Museum featuring contemporary and traditional crafts and the María Poveka Martínez Museum as well as or the pueblo's January 23$^{rd}$ feast day that opens with a dawn Animal Dance.

San Ildefonso Pueblo is on New Mexico 502 northwest of Santa Fe. A self-guided walking tour begins at the Visitor and Information Center and includes visits to San Ildefonso artists' shops. The Visitor Center also sells maps and permits for noncommercial photography. There is no fee to enter the pueblo.

## SAN JUAN PUEBLO

Pueblo de San Juan de los Caballeros is the Spanish name for one of the surviving New Mexico pueblos. In 2005, residents reverted to the traditional name, Ohkay Owingeh. The main entry has directions and additional details.

## SAN JUAN RIVER RUINS

South of Bluff, Utah the San Juan River passes a number of Ancestral Puebloan sites. Most are small hamlets with associated granaries and rock art panels. Although older sites have been discovered in the area, most of the visible structures date from the 13$^{th}$ century.

Most sites are not accessible from the land and seasonal river rafting is the most practical way to visit them. On occasion, the Crow Canyon Archaeological Center arranges trips for its members and several commercial outfitters are listed on the Utah Guides and Outfitters Web page www.utahguidesandoutfitter.com

## SAN MARCOS PUEBLO

San Marcos Pueblo south of Santa Fe, New Mexico is a remnant of a large Ancestral Puebloan community occupied around 1300 to 1680 A.D. Archeologists have identified several large room blocks built around a central plaza with numerous kivas. Estimates place the total number of rooms between 3,000 and 5,000.

Founded by immigrants from the four corners area, San Marcos Pueblo was the largest village in the Galisteo Basin. It was the community center for other villages in the area and became an important campsite on the El Camino Real de Tierra Adentro. Following the Pueblo Revolt of 1680, inhabitants fled to Arizona.

San Marcos Pueblo is not open to the public. Occasionally public tours are offered and you may contact the Archeological Conservancy for additional information.

## ☙ SAND CANYON PUEBLO

Sand Canyon Pueblo was a well-fortified village built around the head of Sand Canyon. Originally, there were structures on both sides and down the east face to the canyon floor below. All were surrounded by a defensive wall with watchtowers reminiscent of a medieval castle.

Today, the structures have collapsed, but the site tells us much about the stress and turmoil that engulfed the Ancestral Puebloans during the thirteenth century. Originally built over a thirty-year period beginning around 1240, the Pueblo was abandoned by about 1285 following a catastrophic attack that killed many of the residents. Significantly, there is no evidence of foreign attackers and archeologists believe people from local villages destroyed Sand Canyon in a bid to control natural resources.

At first glance, there is little to see. Overgrown rubble mounds mark the site and modern excavators reburied the structures and contoured the land to resemble its natural appearance. However, Sand Canyon was a large site with at least 420 rooms, 100 kivas, and 14 towers. You will see stubs of a few standing walls and a bit of imagination is needed to enjoy your visit. Today, a comfortable walking trail guides you around and through the site and six interpretive signs explain how the pueblo was organized, what it may have looked like and how people lived in the arid environment.

Sand Canyon Pueblo is now part of Canyons of the Ancients National Monument and you should begin your visit at the Anasazi Heritage Center in Dolores, Colorado. The entry fee is modest and center staff will provide directions, information about current road conditions, and an informative brochure. A considerably more detailed guide is available for download from www.AnasaziAdventure.com. Services at the site are limited to a small parking area shared with the northern end of the Sand Canyon Trail. There is no water, toilet or phone and the site is not wheelchair accessible.

## ☙ SAND CANYON TRAIL

The Sand Canyon Trail northwest of Cortez, Colorado offers one of the most pleasant hikes in the southwest. End to end, the trail is just over six miles long and descends gradually from 6,800 feet elevation in the north to 5,400 feet at the south. Most of the elevation change is confined to the northern quarter of the trail and portions are steep. This end of the trail can be treacherous following rain or snow, but the entire route is well marked. Worn paths through piñon-juniper forest predominate while the southern part crosses slick rock marked with stone cairns.

Views of Sleeping Ute Mountain as well as small fertile washes are part of the Trail's charm, but the real highlights are partially stabilized Ancestral Puebloan sites along the way. Saddlehorn Hamlet is typical while Sand Canyon and Castle Rock Pueblos anchor the northern and southern ends.

Many experienced hikers leave a vehicle at the southern end and hike from north to south before driving back to pick up their first. Other hikers enjoy shorter in-and-out walks from either end.

*A small ruin found along Sand Canyon Trail. Photo by Eric Skopec*

The Sand Canyon Trail is part of Canyons of the Ancients National Monument. First time visitors should begin their excursions at the Anasazi Heritage Center to pick up a map and get information about current conditions. Please see the Anasazi Heritage Center entry for directions and other information.

## SAND ISLAND PETROGLYPH SITE

The Sand Island Petroglyph Site is a cliff face along the San Juan River 2 miles west of Bluff, Utah. Many glyphs date from the Ancestral Puebloan occupation—roughly 1100 to 1300 A.D., but others are associated with Archaic people and may be 3,000 years old. Representative images include Kokopelli, bighorn sheep, human feet, snakes and geometric figures commonly called zig-zags.

*Ancestral Puebloan petroglyphs. Photo courtesy of www.riparian.smugmug.com*

Today, the glyph panels share the area with a Bureau of Land Management campground and launching ramp. To reach the site from Bluff, drive west on US 163/191 and turn left of Sand Island Road. Drive straight between the campground and launching ramp and park on the dirt pull out next to a talus slope. Follow the well-worn trails to the glyph panels overlooking the river.

## SANTA ANA PUEBLO

Santa Ana Pueblo is among the least traditional of the 19 New Mexico pueblos and has taken the greatest advantage of economic opportunities afforded by its proximity to Albuquerque. Commercial endeavors include two golf courses, a casino and the Ta-Ma-Ya Cooperative Association selling traditional crafts.

Oral histories maintain that the people have lived in the region since sometime before 1500 A.D. The original village was destroyed in the Pueblo Revolt of 1680 and survivors resettled the area in 1693. They reacquired some adjacent lands and agriculture was the primary activity until the tribe began to diversify in the 1980s. Tamaya, the Old Santa Ana Pueblo, is open to the public only on designated feast days and photography, sketching and recording are not allowed. Other villages are more accessible and the rest of the pueblo is open daily for visitation. Ceremonial dances open to the public are conducted in June and July and the annual feast day honoring the Pueblo's patron saint, Saint Ann, is celebrated on July 26th.

Santa Ana Pueblo is adjacent to Highway 550 approximately 25 miles northwest of Albuquerque. Public services are most readily available in nearby Bernalillo, New Mexico.

## ❦❦ SANTA CLARA PUEBLO

Santa Clara Pueblo is home to descendents of the people who occupied the Puye Cliff Dwellings. Built in the mid 16th century, the historic village features one- and two-story adobe houses surrounding two main plazas, rectangular kivas and an early 20th century church.

Today, Santa Clara Pueblo is noted for carved blackware pottery and spectacular natural beauty. Recreational activities include picnicking, fishing and camping—all by permit—plus tours through the historic pueblo. Visitors are free to wander the pueblo from dawn to dusk and some community festivals are open to the public. St. Anthony's Feast Day in June and Harvest Dances and Corn Dances in August are especially appealing.

The Santa Clara Pueblo is 1 mile south of Española on New Mexico 30. There is no admission charge but visitors may be asked to contribute to preservation projects.

## ❦❦ SANTO DOMINGO PUEBLO

Santo Domingo Pueblo is one of the most traditional of the 19 New Mexico pueblos. Many men and women wear traditional hairstyles and maintain their ancient religious structures and societies as well as their native language, Kersan.

Located along the ancient trade round between Albuquerque and Santa Fe, the Pueblo was a headquarters for Spanish missions in the area. Subsequent influxes of tourists have produced a thriving craft industry and Santo Domingo pottery and silver-turquoise jewelry are among the most sought after. In addition, many traditional ceremonies are open to visitors and the Annual Feast of Saint Dominic on August 4th draws dancers from many of the other pueblos.

Santo Domingo Pueblo is on New Mexico Highway 22 off Interstate 25 at a well-signed exit. A cultural center and small museum orient visitors to the pueblo and numerous roadside stands sell authentic jewelry, pottery and silverwork. There is no admission fee but donations to the museum are appreciated.

## ❦❦ SEARS-KAY SITE

The Sears-Kay Site near Carefree, Arizona is the remnant of a Hohokam village occupied between 1050 and 1200 A.D. It consists of 40 rooms in four compounds atop a hill which affords a 360 degree view of the surrounding landscape.

Although the site has only been partially stabilized, many walls stand 3 feet high and it is easy to visualize rooms and the living community of which they were a part. Well-placed interpretive signs add to the experience.

The hike to the site from the parking area is a one mile round trip on a smooth, well-worn trail. The elevation gain is a little over 300 feet and the trail is steep in places. Visitors should be alert for snakes, bees and wasps and protect themselves from the intense sun.

Most of the drive to the Sears-Kay Site is on paved roads, but the final mile or so may require a high clearance, four-wheel drive vehicle following heavy precipitation. From Carefree, drive east on Cave Creek Road, which becomes Seven Springs Road. Turn at Forest Service Road 24 and pull into the graded parking area.

## SHERWOOD RANCH PUEBLO

Previously known as the Raven Site, the Sherwood Ranch Pueblo is the remnant of an Ancestral Puebloan village near St. Johns, Arizona. It sits on a low hill overlooking the Little Colorado River and was occupied from about 900 A.D. into the mid 16th Century.

Surveys indicate that the pueblo had between 250 and 400 rooms, but the site has been heavily damaged. Pothunters mined the site for artifacts and a commercial endeavor known as the White Mountain Archeological Center excavated, stabilized and partially reconstructed the site without documenting the work.

In 2002, the property's owners terminated lease agreements with White Mountain and donated the site to the Archaeological Conservancy. Beginning in 2003, the Conservancy mapped and reburied the site and renamed it the Sherwood Ranch Pueblo in honor of Ruth and Wendel Sherwood who donated it.

The site is not open to casual visitors and Arizona Site Stewards monitor traffic. The Archaeological Conservancy can arrange guided tours for interested groups.

## SHOOFLY VILLAGE RUINS

Shoofly Village Ruins near Payson, Arizona are the remains of a Hohokam village occupied between 1000 and 1250 A.D. Situated atop one edge of Houston Mesa, the village had nearly 90 rooms and covered almost 4 acres surrounded by a low stone wall.

Pothunters have done a great deal of damage at the site and removed large quantities of artifacts. Professional excavations in the 1980s recovered considerable information and reburied large portions of the site. Today, a self-guided interpretive trail leads visitors through the ruins and most structures are visible as low walls outlining individual rooms.

Shoofly Village Ruins is about 5 miles north of Payson. From Payson, drive north on Highway 87 and turn right, east on Houston Mesa Road. You will pass through the Mesa del Caballo subdivision to a parking area just off the paved road. Services at the site are limited to picnic tables, shade ramadas and toilets, but there is no admission fee.

## SNAKETOWN

Snaketown was an important Hohokam village occupied from roughly 200 B.C. through the early 15th century A.D. Located in the lower Gila River valley near Chandler, Arizona, Snaketown was the site of important archeological research and is frequently mentioned in specialist and popular literature.

First excavated in 1934, Snaketown was re-excavated in the mid 1960s. Archeologists identified more than 60 middens in an area a little over 1/3 square mile. They also recognized the remains of numerous pit houses surrounding a central plaza, two Mesoamerican style ball courts and an extensive irrigation system. The population may have been as large as 2,000 people.

Snaketown was designated a National Historic Landmark in 1964, but the site is not open to the public and excavated features were reburied to protect them for future research.

Please see the Hohokam Pima National Monument entry for additional information.

## ᭐᭐᭐ TAOS PUEBLO

Taos Pueblo is among the best known of the 19 surviving New Mexico pueblos. About 25 miles north of Santa Fe, the principal structures were built around 1450 A.D. and now appear much as they did when the Spanish entered the southwest in 1540. Taos Pueblo is among the oldest continuously occupied communities in the United States.

Today, the pueblo occupies 99,000 acres with a population of nearly 5,000. About 150 residents live full time in the old village. Surrounded by a wall which defines the community's boundaries, the north and south buildings stand five stories tall and feature adobe walls several feet thick at the base. The north structure is one of the most photographed buildings in North America.

Residents of the old village maintain their traditions and do not use electricity or indoor plumbing. They ask visitors to respect their privacy, but the village is open from 8 a.m. to 4 p.m. Monday through Saturday and 8:30 a.m. to 4:30 p.m. on Sundays. The pueblo closes for traditional ceremonies several times a year, but public dances are held on December 25th, Deer Dances; January 1st, Turtle Dance; and January 6th, Buffalo Dances. Well-signed shops sell arts and crafts as well as traditional foods.

The admission fee is $10 for adults, $5 for students and children under 13 are free. There is a $5 fee for noncommercial still photography. The old village is 1 mile north of the modern community of Taos, New Mexico at a signed exit from US Highway 64.

## ᭐᭐ TESUQUE PUEBLO

Tesuque Pueblo near Santa Fe, New Mexico was built by immigrants from the four corners region. It has occupied its current location since 1200 A.D. and its residents are among the most conservative puebloans. Although listed on the National Register of Historic Places, the pueblo does not allow photography.

The Pueblo closes regularly for traditional ceremonies, but a few are open to the public. The annual Feast Day of San Diego on November 12th, the Christmas Day Celebration, the Three Kings Day festivities in January and the Corn Dance on the first weekend in June are the most popular. In addition, resident artists produce brightly colored pottery based upon traditional designs and beautifully modeled figurines that are considered to be collectors items. There is a gift store at the Camel Rock Casino operated by the tribe and many items are sold at the Tesuque Pueblo Flea Market on Opera Hill every weekend from February to December.

Tesuque Pueblo is 9 miles north of Santa Fe on Highway 85/285 and the exit is well signed. There is no fee to enter the pueblo and most services are available at the nearby Camel Rock Casino.

## ᭐᭐ THREE KIVA PUEBLO

Also known as "Three Kiva Ruins," Three Kiva Pueblo is a small Bureau of Land Management interpretive site near Monticello in southeastern Utah. The principal structure is a 14-room pueblo occupied between 1000 and 1300 A.D. The structure has been partially reconstructed and one kiva may be entered by a ladder.

*Three Rivers Petroglyhs Site. Photo courtesy of James Pickrell (www.pathfinder.smugmug.com)*

The site is along Montezuma Canyon Road about 15 miles north of Hatch Trading Post and 23 miles south of the road's intersection with US Hwy 163. There are no services at the site and admission is free.

## ❧❧❧ THREE RIVERS PETROGLYPHS SITE

Three Rivers Petroglyphs Site near Tularosa, New Mexico contains more than 21,000 Mogollon petroglyphs. Carved between 900 and 1400 A.D., the glyphs depict people, birds, animals, fish, insects and plants as well as geometric or abstract designs.

Today, a rough trail leads from the visitors' shelter into a large concentration of glyphs. The round trip is just over a mile long and a detailed guide is available at the site. The remains of a small pueblo are nearby.

To reach the Site, turn east from US Highway 54 at Three Rivers onto County Road B30 for five miles. The road is paved and signs point the way. The day use fee is $2 and there are 5 shelters, restrooms and drinking water as well as two RV sites.

## ❧❧ TIJERAS PUEBLO ARCHEOLOGICAL SITE

Tijeras Pueblo near Tijeras, New Mexico was the principal structure in an Ancestral Puebloan community formed by immigrants from the four corners region. Initially created shortly after 1300 A.D., the pueblo consisted of 200 rooms in a U shape around a central plaza. Numerous smaller structures nearby are evidenced by mounds and depressions. The pueblo has been excavated several times and refilled afterward.

Today it appears to be little more than a large mound, but excavations have revealed much of its story. Around 1368 A.D., the pueblo was abandoned for about two decades. People returned around 1390 A.D. and as many as 400 lived here for the next 35 years. The site was finally abandoned around 1425 A.D.

An easy self-guided interpretive trail leads through the site. Signs along the 1/3 mile trail point out key features and help visitors visualize the living pueblo. In addition, summer workshops include drum and pottery making as well as flint knapping. A new interpretive center with multimedia educational stations and a hands-on work area is being built and will raise the rating on Tijeras Pueblo to 3 stars.

Tijeras Pueblo is located behind the Sandia Ranger District Office at 11776 Highway 337, 1/2 mile north of Interstate 40. The self-guided trail is open from 8 a.m. to 5 p.m. on weekdays and from 8:30 a.m. to 5 p.m. on weekends. There is no fee to enter the site but donations are appreciated.

## ❧❧ TONTO NATIONAL MONUMENT

Tonto National Monument preserves Salado sites in the heart of the Tonto Basin, between Payson and Globe, Arizona. Many sites were submerged beneath Roosevelt Lake, but the Monument preserves two hillside villages that are open to the public.

The "lower" ruin is a pueblo-like structure on a low rise adjacent to the Visitors' Center. A self-guided interpretive trail leads visitors through the structure that once had 19 rooms. The adjoining annex added another 12 rooms. The larger "upper" ruin is a partially stabilized cliff dwelling that had as many as 40 rooms. It can be visited only on ranger-

*Upper Ruin, Tonto National Monument. Photo by Eric Skopec*

guided hikes. The round trip is just over three miles with a modest elevation gain and groups are limited to 15. Reservations are required and you can call ahead to reserve a spot: (520) 467-2241.

The Monument is located on a well-signed side road off Arizona Highway 88 and open daily except Christmas from 8 a.m. to 5 p.m. Guided tours of the Upper Ruin are offered November through April, but the number of tours depends on staffing. The Visitors' Center museum displays artifacts recovered from sites in and around the Monument and facilities are limited to a picnic area, restrooms, vending machines and a public telephone. Admission is $3 per person.

### ᎳᎳ TSANKAWI RUINS

Tsankawi Ruins near Los Alamos, New Mexico is the centerpiece of a detached unit of Bandelier National Monument. Archeological evidence shows that the area had been sparsely occupied prior to 1300 A.D., but the population swelled with immigrants from the four corners area. People of both Chacoan and Mesa Verdean origins contributed to the growth and apparently lived here in peace for over two centuries.

Built in the early 1400s, Tsankawi pueblo was a rectangular stone structure around a central courtyard. With approximately 350 rooms, the structure stood three stories tall and overlooked surrounding canyons from its position on a mesa.

Today, a short but steep trail leads from the parking area to the site. The trail extends down the "back" of the site to cave-like structures built into the cliff and numerous petro-

*Ranger talk at the Tusayan Museum. Visitors learn about the early people who made Grand Canyon their home 800 years ago. National Park Service photo.*

glyphs can be seen along the 1.5 mile round trip. The interpretive brochure highlights features along the way including points where the trail is worn deeply into the soft stone.

Although its not necessary, first-time visitors will benefit by stopping at the Bandelier National Monument visitors' center. Please see the main entry for directions and additional information.

## TUSAYAN RUIN

The Grand Canyon is a 6,000-foot deep cleft carved by the Colorado River. The National Park protects some of the most arresting scenery in North America. Ancient peoples may have been as awed by its beauty as we are, but they also built homes here and exploited the Canyon's natural resources. More than 4,300 archeological sites have been cataloged within the park boundaries.

Tusayan Ruin is the most accessible and one of the best-preserved archeological sites in the Park. It is a remnant of a small Ancestral Puebloan village occupied by about 30 people for three decades in the late 1100s. Exposed portions include a kiva, plaza and grain storage areas. Smaller than great pueblos and less spectacular than cliff dwellings, Tusayan Ruin is typical of small villages and unit pueblos that dotted the Ancestral Puebloan homeland during the 11th and 12th centuries.

Tusayan Ruin is located three miles west of Desert View and is open daily 9 a.m. to 5 p.m. There is no additional admission fee but the site is only accessible by free shuttle bus, a one-mile walk or bicycle ride from Market Plaza on the Greenway Trail, or a short walk from Mather Point. At the site, a level self-guiding trail winds through the pueblo and to an adjacent museum that houses artifacts recovered during excavation.

*Tuzigoot National Monument. Photo by Eric Skopec*

Grand Canyon National Park is approximately 60 miles north of Interstate Highway 40 and well-signed routes near Flagstaff and Williams, Arizona lead you directly to the south rim Visitor's Center. Snow closures may affect your drive during winter months and you can call toll-free for current conditions: (888) 411-ROAD—(888)411-7623. There is an admission fee and high demand for lodging and other services during peak visitation times.

## ❧❧ TUZIGOOT NATIONAL MONUMENT

Tuzigoot National Monument preserves the remains of an 80 or more room Sinagua and Hohokam village occupied between 1125 and 1400 A.D. Located near Cottonwood, Arizona the three-story pueblo sits atop a low hill partially surrounded by a gentle bend in the Verde River.

Two hundred people may have lived in the pueblo and there were probably other structures nearby. Modern development has obscured related sites and farming fields, but the pueblo itself was stabilized by the Civilian Conservation Corp and archaeologists believe 90% of the remaining structure is authentic. First excavated in the 1930s, Tuzigoot was a treasure trove of artifacts and more than 22,000 pieces are stored in the Visitors' Center Museum.

The Monument is open daily from 8 a.m. to 6 p.m. during summer months. It closes an hour earlier during the winter and is closed on Christmas Day. Admission is $5 and children under 16 are free. Services at the Visitors' Center are limited, but food and lodging are available in neighboring communities.

## ❦❦ UNIVERSITY OF COLORADO MUSEUM OF NATURAL HISTORY

The University of Colorado Museum of Natural History in Boulder, Colorado houses more than 1.5 million southwestern artifacts and nearly 50,000 photographs. Highlights include a textile collection, Navajo and Pueblo silverwork and kachina dolls as well as the papers of Earl H. Morris, Anna O. Shepard, and Joe Ben Wheat. A permanent exhibit explains the techniques researchers use to understand the lives of Ancestral Puebloan, Navajo, Zuni and Hopi peoples. Recent temporary exhibitions have focused on Corn Mother Traditions and some controversies about evolution.

The Museum is on the University of Colorado Campus in the Henderson Building between 15th and 16th streets just east of Broadway. The Museum is open from 9 a.m. to 5 p.m. on weekdays and 9 a.m. to 4 p.m. on Saturdays and Sundays. There is no admission fee but the suggested donation is $3 for adults and $1 for children and seniors. Paid parking is available in the immediate area.

## ❦ UTE MOUNTAIN TRIBAL PARK

The Ute Mountain Tribal Park is adjacent to Mesa Verde National Park and contains many magnificent cliff dwellings in the Mesa Verde tradition. Lion House, Hoot Owl House and the Nordenskiold Cliff Dwelling are among the infrequently visited sites within the Park.

Hours of operation are irregular and guests may enter the Park only when accompanied by a Ute Tribal guide. Guides offer full- and half-day tours and fees vary with the number of people in the group. Most visitors drive their own vehicles, but guides can provide transportation with advance notice and additional fees. From time to time, guides offer special tours of remote, seldom visited areas including the Nordenskiold Cliff Dwelling.

The tribal headquarters and museum are located in Towaoc, Colorado, southwest of Cortez. The tribe's Web site invites visitors to email for additional information, but you are more likely to get a response by calling (800) 749-1452.

## ❦❦ V-BAR-V HERITAGE SITE

The V-Bar-V Heritage Site protects the largest known petroglyph site in the Verde Valley of Arizona. Earlier generations of visitors have damaged parts of the panel but the Forest Service has protected it since 1994. Representatives of the Verde Valley Archaeological Society and Friends of the Forest conduct guided tours during operating hours.

The site is open from 9 a.m. to 3 p.m. Friday, Saturday, Sunday and Monday year round but closed on Thanksgiving and Christmas day. There is a small Visitors' Center and bookstore near the parking area along with chemical toilets. A Red Rock Pass is required to visit the V-Bar-V Heritage Site and you will receive directions when you pick up your pass.

## ❦ VILLAGE OF GREAT KIVAS

Village of the Great Kivas on the Zuni Reservation in New Mexico is the remnant of a modest Ancestral Puebloan settlement. Largely unexcavated, the site includes an 18-room pueblo along with two great kivas.

*Rooms in alcoves at Walnut Canyon National Monument. Photo by Eric Skopec*

The Zuni consider the site to be part of their cultural heritage and ask interested people to contact the tribal office before attempting to visit; (505) 782-4481

### VISTA DEL RIO CULTURAL RESOURCE PARK

Vista del Rio Cultural Resource Park in Tucson, Arizona preserves undisturbed portions of a large Hohokam village occupied between 1000 and 1200 A.D. Much of the village site has been destroyed by modern development, but test excavations within the park revealed concentrations of artifacts, well-preserved pit houses, outlines of an above-ground structure, outdoor storage and roasting pits and remnants of an irrigation canal.

The Park is located at 1575 East Desert Arbor Street, north of Tanque Verde Road between Sabino Canyon Road and the Pantano/Wrightstown Roads interchange. The Park is open from dawn to dusk and amenities include a ramada, walking trail and interpretive signs. There is no admission fee.

### WALNUT CANYON NATIONAL MONUMENT

Walnut Canyon is a 20-mile long gash southeast of Flagstaff, Arizona. Averaging a quarter mile wide and as much as 400 feet deep, the Canyon's ledges were home to a group of Sinagua from 1120 to 1250 A.D. The National Monument protects more than 300 dwellings built into sheltered overhangs along an 8-mile stretch of the canyon.

Two self-guided trails lead visitors to overlooks and entries to about 100 rooms. The shorter, and less demanding Rim Trail is under a mile long and features two canyon overlooks plus a pit house and pueblo set back from the canyon rim. The longer Island Trail descends 185 feet into the canyon and provides a close view of 25 cliff dwellings. This is a strenuous 1-mile round trip that involves climbing the 240 steps back up to the Visitors' Center level.

The Monument is about 10 miles southeast of Flagstaff along Interstate Highway 40. Exit 204 is well signed and brings travelers to the Visitors' Center. The Monument is open daily from 8 a.m. to 6 p.m. (summer) or 9 a.m. to 5 p.m. (winter) except Christmas day. Admission is $5 but children under 16 are free. The park entrance and both trails close an hour before the Monument.

### ᘐᘐ WESTERN NEW MEXICO UNIVERSITY MUSEUM

Western New Mexico University Museum in Silver City, New Mexico houses nearly 2,000 Native American Artifacts including basketry, footwear, stone artifacts and shaped bone tools dating from Paleo-Indian times through around 1500 A.D. In addition, the permanent display of Mimbres Pottery is one of the largest in the world.

The Museum is located in Fleming Hall on the Western New Mexico University Campus at 1000 W. College St. There is no admission fee and it is open from 9 a.m. to 4:30 p.m. Monday through Friday and 10 a.m. to 4 p.m. on weekends. It is closed on University holidays.

### ᘐᘐ WESTWATER RUIN

Westwater Ruin near Blanding, Utah is the remains of a heavily damaged Ancestral Puebloan village along Westwater Creek. Occupied between 1150 and 1275 A.D., the site had about 13 dwelling rooms, 5 kivas, storage structures and outdoor work areas. Also known as the Five Kiva Ruin, the site has suffered from a century of pot hunting and vandalism but still offers an attractive vista.

From Blanding, drive south about 1 mile on Highway 191 and right on County Road 232 which is labeled "Ruin Road" on some maps. The overlook is about two miles from the intersection.

### WHITE MOUNTAIN ARCHEOLOGICAL CENTER

The White Mountain Archeological Center was formed to preserve an Ancestral Puebloan village dubbed the Raven Site. The Center's founders intended to support operations by charging fees to visit or participate in excavations.

The White Mountain Archeological Center closed abruptly in the 1990s, but it had been heavily promoted and you may still see references to it. Today, the Raven Site is owned by the Archeological Conservancy and has been renamed the Sherwood Ranch Pueblo in honor of Wendel and Ruth Sherwood who donated the land.

### ᘐᘐᘐ WUPATKI NATIONAL MONUMENT

Wupatki National Monument near Flagstaff, Arizona protects more than 2,700 archeological sites within its 54 square miles. Most visible structures were built by the Sinagua, but the archeological record is divided by the eruption of Sunset Crater in 1064 A.D. Prior to the eruption, Wupatki was home to the Northern Sinagua. Their population was decimated by the explosion and the area was reoccupied a decade later by Southern Sinagua and Hohokam immigrants.

*Wupatki Pueblo. Photo by Eric Skopec*

Today, you can visit six principal sites. From the Visitors' Center, a paved trail leads to the three-story Wupatki Pueblo. A large Hohokam-style ball court here emphasizes the influence of southern people during the Pueblo's heyday. Other sites are visited by driving north from the Visitors' Center and stopping at well marked parking areas. Short walks averaging about half a mile are required to visit Wukoki, Nalakihu, Citadel and Lomaki Pueblos as well as the Box Canyon Dwellings.

Wupatki National Monument is on a road paralleling US Highway 89 east of Flagstaff, Arizona. The loop is shared with Sunset Crater Volcano National Monument and the $5 admission fee covers admission to both Monuments. The individual pass is good for 7 days and children under 16 are free. The Visitors' Center is open from 9 a.m. to 5 p.m. daily but is closed on Christmas day.

## YELLOW JACKET PUEBLO

Yellow Jacket Pueblo was one of the largest Ancestral Puebloan villages in the Mesa Verde Region. People occupied the site for two and a half centuries beginning around 1050 A.D. Archeological surveys have identified surface features on more than 100 acres. Nearly 195 kivas, 1,200 surface rooms, 19 towers and a probable Chaco-style great house have been noted.

Yellow Jacket is frequently mentioned in relevant literature, but the site is not open for visitation. For the curious, site reports from several excavations are available online at http://yellowjacket.colorado.edu and http://www.crowcanyon.org/publications/yellow_ jacket_pueblo.asp.

## ❀❀ YUCCA HOUSE NATIONAL MONUMENT

Yucca House National Monument protects an unexcavated pueblo occupied by the Ancestral Puebloans from 1150 to 1300 A.D. It was one of the largest sites in the area and probably had more that 600 rooms and 100 kivas divided into two principal structures.

The "West Complex" is the larger of the two and includes a great kiva that may have served the whole community. The "Lower House" is considerably smaller with only eight ground floor rooms and an enclosed plaza. Today, brush covers most of the site and few standing walls are visible. There is little to hold the attention of first-time visitors, but those with more experience will recognize outlines of the pueblo, mounds covering associated structures, a spring flowing through the middle and Ancestral Puebloan fields still cultivated by modern residents.

Yucca House is located southwest of Cortez, Colorado on County Road B. Signage is poor but most local residents can provide directions. There are no services or stewards at the site, but you can download a site guide at http://www.nps.gov/yuho/historyculture/index.htm.

## ZIA PUEBLO

Founded around 1250 A.D. by immigrants from Chaco Canyon, Zia Pueblo sits atop a small mesa west of Bernalillo, New Mexico. With a population of fewer than 1,000 people, Zia is among the smallest pueblos. Residents welcome tourists with an uncommercialized view of pueblo life and there are few visitor services.

Visitors are asked to check in at the Tribal office when they arrive, but are otherwise free to wander narrow lanes during daylight hours. Highlights include the charming whitewashed cobblestone and mud houses, the old church, Nuestra Señora de la Asuncíon decorated with yellow and white horses painted by a local artist and a white cross in the plaza where residents were baptized after the Spanish reconquest in 1692. Zia potters are known for the use of geometric designs and the Pueblo is the home of the sun symbol which adorns the New Mexico state flag.

Zia Pueblo is just a mile off Highway 550 and the exit is well-signed. The small Zia Cultural Center sells pottery, paintings, sculpture and weavings while representatives in the Tribal Office are pleased to answer questions and provide directions.

## ZION NATIONAL PARK

Zion National Park near Springdale, Utah is noted for its natural beauty. Favorite visitor activities include bicycling, bird watching, hiking, horseback riding and nature photography.

Although archeological sites are not a principal feature of the park, there is abundant evidence of ancient peoples. Artifacts, rock art panels and scattered campsites show that Archaic and Fremont people used the Park's resources and Ancestral Puebloans built several permanent habitations. Today, artifacts gathered by Rangers and other people are displayed in the museum one half mile north of the park's south entrance. In addition, a recently excavated food storage area near the Visitors' Center is open to the public. Dubbed the Watchman Archeological Site, the spot was used to dry, hull, grind and store corn and wild seeds. In addition to three storage cysts, archeologists uncovered two storage rooms, 2 fire hearths and nearly 1,600 artifacts including stone tools and pottery fragments. Coincidentally, only about 14% of the Park has been formally surveyed and additional sites are likely to be discovered as work continues.

*Zion Canyon as viewed from Angels Landing. National Park Service photo*

Zion is located in southwest Utah and Visitors Centers are accessible from both Interstate Highway 15 and Highway 9. Both are open daily, except Christmas, from 8 a.m. Closing hours vary with the season; 4:30 or 5 p.m. in the winter, later at other times of the year. The Human History Museum is open daily except Christmas and staff at either Visitors Center can provide the current hours. The admission fee is $25 per private vehicle, good for 7 days, and services are available in proximate communities—Springdale, Rockville, Mt. Carmel Junction, Kanab—and the Zion Lodge along the canyon scenic drive.

### ZUNI PUEBLO

Zuni Pueblo was the first Native American community visited by the Spanish in 1540. Descendents of the Ancestral Puebloans built Zuni at the start of the 14th century and the numerous archeological sites from the same era testify to a population boom as Ancestral Puebloans relocated to the area. Coincidentally, the Zuni consider the abandoned sites to be sacred homes of their ancestors.

Today, Zuni is an artists' colony and nearly 90% of local families are involved in the production of inlayed silver jewelry, stone fetishes, pottery and weavings. Their work is world famous and visitors can buy fine pieces directly from the artisans or at the many trading posts nearby. Located a few miles south of Interstate Highway 40 and about 140 miles west of Albuquerque, Zuni is a sovereign nation with its own government, court system and police force. There is no fee to enter the Pueblo, but you should check in at the Visitor Center when you arrive. Remember, Zuni is a living community, not a museum, and you should respect the residents' privacy. The A:shiwi A:wan Museum and Heritage Center have exhibits explaining the Pueblo's history and culture. For a fee, experienced Zuni guides conduct tours of the Spanish mission, original Pueblo, and artists' studios. Lodging includes a bed and breakfast in the heart of Zuni as well as numerous motels, restaurants, and an RV park in nearby Gallup, New Mexico.

# SUGGESTED
# ADVENTURES

*Wooden ladder at Bandelier National Monument. National Park Service photo by Sally King*

## SECTIONS

With so many interesting places to visit, planning a vacation in the southwest can be a daunting task. The list of "must see" sites and indexes by location and culture will simplify your work and the suggested adventures in the following few pages may help even more.

Each adventure is planned for five or six active days and you can expand or contract them to fit your needs and interests. Notice that the directions are a bit sketchy. I assume that you travel with a good road map and the American Automobile Association's Indian Country Map is the best I've found.

Directions, road names or numbers and approximate distances are correct as of this writing. Road and traffic condition can change quickly. Allow extra time to avoid needless stress, and, if you are ever in doubt, check with knowledgeable people in the local area.

Please remember that these itineraries worked for me. Your interests—and those of your companions—may differ. Feel free to modify these suggestions as you wish, bypass less interesting sites and add others that you find intriguing.

Finally, budgets may force some parks to close or reduce their operating hours. There is a list of travel advisories on our Web page, www.AnasaziAdventure.com and you can help keep it updated. If you encounter situations you hadn't expected, please email details to updates@AnasaziAdventure.com

# THE GOLDEN CIRCLE TOUR

Ancestral Puebloan culture grew up in the four corners area and driving an extended loop called the Golden Circle that will bring you to many of their most spectacular sites. This itinerary involves driving just over 550 miles mostly on good, paved roads.

Depending on your level of activity, you can visit as many as 30 sites including 10 "must see" spots. Collectively, the sites represent about 1,500 years of Ancestral Puebloan development beginning with pit houses, extending through unit pueblos, and concluding with massive pueblos and exotic cliff houses.

The Golden Circle begins near Albuquerque, New Mexico, the major transportation hub in the area, but you can start at any point along the route. If you begin in Albuquerque you can visit the Maxwell Museum or the Pueblo Cultural Center and find lodging north of the city along Highway 550. There are a few motels in Cuba, New Mexico but more are available further back along the route around Bernalillo.

## DAY 1 CHACO CULTURE NATIONAL HISTORIC PARK

Chaco Canyon was home to the most fully integrated branch of the Ancestral Puebloan family. Today, visitors can walk through a half dozen great houses, visit a massive great kiva, and hike trails overlooking the canyon floor.

The signed route to Chaco exits Highway 550 just a mile south of Nageezi and includes seventeen miles of graded dirt. The route is typically passable but be cautious after heavy rain or snow. Allow an hour for the final leg even in good weather.

*A rare tri-wall structure can be found among the ruins at Aztec Ruins National Monument. Only a dozen such structures have been discovered among Ancestral Puebloan ruins. Photo by Chris Skopec*

Plan to arrive at the Visitors' Center around 9 a.m. when it opens. The Center hosts a small museum as well as an orientation video and helpful rangers will be pleased to help you plan your visit.

There is a great deal to see in Chaco, but you should leave around 4 p.m. Be sure to stop at the Fajada Butte overlook on your way out. Return to Highway 550 and drive north to Bloomfield, New Mexico about 50 miles north of Nageezi. Lodging is generally available at a handful of motels. In the worst case, many more are available in nearby Farmington.

## DAY 2 SALMON AND AZTEC RUINS

The Chacoans moved north when they abandoned the Canyon and today's route follows their footsteps. Have a good breakfast and spend the morning at the Salmon Ruins in Bloomfield. The ruined pueblo is less imposing than others you will see, but the museum is among the best in the southwest.

When you finish at Salmon, drive north to Aztec, about 10 miles away. There are several restaurants in the heart of the community and my personal favorite is the Bistro. If you happen to stop there, please say "hello" to Tony, the owner, for me.

Aztec Ruins National Monument is just a mile or two from the middle of town. One of the great houses at Aztec has been fully excavated and others form clearly defined mounds. A self guided tour leads through a portion of the excavated pueblo with stops at a tri-wall structure and a reconstructed great kiva.

Plan to leave Aztec around 4 p.m. and drive to Mesa Verde, roughly a hundred miles north. With reservations or good luck, you may be able to stay in the Park but more lodging is available in Cortez, Colorado, a dozen miles from the Park entrance. For suggestions, see http://www.mesaverdecountry.com/tourism/lodging.html and book your room for two nights.

## Day 3 Mesa Verde

Mesa Verde National Park features a spectacular collection of cliff dwellings as well as surface structures. It includes 3 "must see" sites in addition to several that come close.

Mesa Verde is a large park and it is difficult to see everything in one day. Get an early start and have a good breakfast before you arrive. Begin your adventure at the Visitors' Center and see if spaces are available on any of the ranger guided tours. There is an extra fee and you need to be in reasonably good physical condition to participate in the tours, but they are the only way to visit some of the most spectacular sites. Plan your stay around the timing of any tours you select and have a light lunch at the concessions in the Park.

Even if you don't join one of the guided tours, there is plenty to see and this will be a full day. At the end of the day, have a nice dinner and return to your lodgings.

## Day 4 Canyons of the Ancients

Canyons of the Ancients is one of our newest national monuments and incorporates several previously established sites. The headquarters is the Anasazi Heritage Center in Dolores, about 20 miles north of Cortez. Start the day with a hearty breakfast and check out of your lodgings.

The Anasazi Heritage Center has a fine museum with a hands-on area that appeals to children and adults alike. It is also proximate to two archeological sites and has several outdoor tables ideal for picnic lunches.

Spend the morning at the Center and get directions to Lowry Pueblo. Lowry began life as a Chacoan outlier and several generations of local people modified it when links to Chaco dissolved. Well-placed interpretive signs help bring the Pueblo to live and the excavated great kiva has some unique features.

When you finish at Lowry, return to Highway 191 and drive south to Chinle, Arizona, about 150 miles away. Lodging is generally available and with luck or reservations you may be able to stay at the Thunderbird Lodge on the edge of Canyon de Chelly National Monument. See http://www.tbirdlodge.com/ for details and book your lodgings for two nights.

## Day 5 Canyon de Chelly

Canyon de Chelly National Monument is a spectacular mix of canyon bottoms and towering red cliffs. Making the most of your visit calls for a little advanced planning.

Without a Navajo guide, you can enter the Visitors' Center, drive the rim roads stopping at well-placed overlooks and hike to White House. With a Navajo guide and a sturdy four-wheel drive vehicle, you can drive into the canyons and walk through numerous sites.

Authorized Navajo guides gather at the Visitors' Center in the morning and generally charge about $10 an hour with a half-day minimum. Alternately, commercial tours are available at the Thunderbird lodge. They fill up quickly during peak season and it may be a good idea to reserve spots when you book a room.

At the end of the day, have a good meal and return to your lodging for a well earned rest.

### DAY 6 HOMEWARD BOUND

From Canyon de Chelly, most people drive south on Highway 191 to Interstate Highway 40, about 80 miles away. If you are returning east, the freeway will take you to Albuquerque, New Mexico, roughly 190 miles and you can easily stop at Acoma or Zuni Pueblos if you have time.

If you are headed west, Interstate 40 will take you to Flagstaff, Arizona, just under 140 miles away. Time permitting, you can visit Petrified Forest National Park, or Walnut Canyon National Monument.

# SANTA FE AND THE NORTHERN RIO GRANDE VALLEY

Espanola in the heart of the northern Rio Grande valley will be your home base for this tour. The town is less well known that Santa Fe, but it is quieter and sits at the junction of major roads leading to a variety of sites. A marked up route map of visits in the area resembles a four-pointed star with Espanola in the middle and arms radiating out to sites of interest.

Founded in 1598, Espanola was the first capital of Spanish New Mexico. Today, it is an emerging artists' colony with a handful of motels and restaurants. Lodgings fill up quickly during peak season and you should call ahead for reservations. I suggest you book for five nights. Check www.espanolaonline.com for a convenient list of motels, restaurants and other services.

To make the best use of your time, try to arrive in Espanola the night before your tours begin.

### DAY 1 COLONIAL SANTA FE

Spend your first day in Santa Fe, 25 miles south of Espanola. The city is built over pueblos founded between 1050 and 1150 A.D., but most ancient traces are buried beneath colonial and modern developments. Most visible structures are reminders of Santa Fe's colonial past.

Begin your day with a good breakfast and allow enough driving time to arrive at the Museum of Indian Arts and Culture when it opens at 10 a.m.. Most people will spend about two hours at the Museum and there are other museums of interest nearby if you have extra time.

*Bandelier National Monumnet. National Park Service photo by Sally King*

After visiting the Museum, find a convenient spot for a light lunch and begin a casual walking tour around the Spanish plaza. Many shops distribute free walking tour guides or you can download one from Frommers, http://www.frommers.com/destinations/san-tafe/0030020033.html. The walk covers about 16 blocks and there is no reason to hurry. Conveniently placed coffee shops and cafes provide plenty of resting places from which you can watch others passing by. At a minimum, your tour should include the Santa Fe Plaza at the heart of the colonial city, the Palace of the Governors, Cathedral Basilica of Saint Francis of Assisi, and the Loretto Chapel noted for its unsupported spiral staircase. You can finish the walk at the San Miguel Mission believed to be the oldest church in the United States. Afterwards, find an engaging restaurant for dinner before returning to your lodgings.

## DAY 2 TAOS PUEBLO

Taos Pueblo is just 45 miles northeast of Espanola. It opens to visitors at 8 a.m. and there is no reason to rush, but photographers may want to arrive early to capture the best light. You will probably want to spend a full day in and around the Pueblo and can enjoy an authentic lunch in small cafes near artists' shops.

## DAY 3 PECOS NATIONAL MONUMENT

Pecos National Monument about 60 miles south east of Espanola is another all-day excursion. If you have the flexibility, visit on Wednesday or Friday, days on which Rangers conduct guided tours of less visited sites within the monument.

Food and other services are available in nearby communities but I usually bring a picnic lunch to enjoy in the Monument.

## DAY 4 SANTA CLARA PUEBLO, PUYE CLIFF DWELLINGS

Santa Clara Pueblo is just about 5 miles south of Espanola on the Los Alamos Highway. Although the distance is short, this will be another all-day excursion when you add in the Puye Cliff Dwellings. Services are available nearby, but this is a great day to pack a picnic lunch and take advantage of the tables available at the Cliff Dwellings.

## DAY 5 BANDELIER NATIONAL MONUMENT

Bandelier National Monument is about 25 miles southwest of Espanola. The pleasant drive will bring you to the detached Tsankawi unit before you reach the main unit. If this is your first visit, bypass Tsankawi and drive directly to the Visitors' Center in the Main Unit. You can stop at Tsankawi on your way home and the visit will be all the more enjoyable once you've had an orientation.

Again, food is available in nearby communities, but this is another good spot for a picnic lunch.

## DAY 6 HOMEWARD BOUND

The visit to Bandelier concludes your northern Rio Grande adventure and you will probably return to Albuquerque, the major transportation hub in the region. Enjoy a leisurely drive stopping where you see things of interest. Cochiti, Santo Domingo, Santa Anna and San Filipe pueblos all have well signed exits from Interstate 25 and you can stop at any that catch your fancy. And once you reach Bernalillo be sure to stop at the Coronado State Monument to visit the partially reconstructed ruins of Kuaua Pueblo.

# FLAGSTAFF, SEDONA AND THE VERDE VALLEY

Flagstaff and Sedona are just 30 miles apart and both are beautiful communities. Flagstaff is a gateway to the Grand Canyon and has the feel of a 19th century village nearly surrounded by snowcapped peaks. Sedona has a "new age" reputation and is a thriving tourist center with art galleries, fine motels and restaurants all surrounded by spectacular red cliffs.

Plan to spend three nights in Flagstaff including the night before you begin touring, and three nights in Sedona. Lodging is readily available in both communities, but many spots fill up quickly during peak season. It's a good idea to make reservations and you can find suggestions at http://www.flagstaffarizona.org/ and http://www.visitsedona.com/. While you are making reservations, you may want to book a commercial jeep tour for Day 5. Many vendors will try to find places for walk-ins, but the tours are popular and you can book in advance with several tour providers listed at http://visitsedona.com/.

*Ruins at Wupatki National Monument. Photo by Eric Skopec*

## DAY 1 MUSEUM OF NORTHERN ARIZONA AND WALNUT CANYON

Begin your day with a hearty breakfast and make your first stop at the Museum of Northern Arizona. It is one of the finest museums in the southwest and features fascinating exhibits, a very good bookstore and exceptionally helpful docents. You can easily spend several hours at the Museum, but there is more to do today. Try to arrive shortly after the museum opens at 9 a.m. and limit your visit to about 90 minutes.

When you leave the Museum, drive east toward Walnut Canyon, about ten miles away. Visit Eldon Pueblo and grab a quick lunch along the way, and spend your afternoon at Walnut Canyon National Monument.

When the Monument closes, have a relaxing dinner and get a good night's rest. There is a bit of walking to do on day 2.

## DAY 2 WUPATKI NATIONAL MONUMENT

Wupatki is less than 50 miles from Flagstaff and the drive will take about an hour under normal conditions. Nevertheless, this is an all-day excursion and it's a good idea to pack a picnic lunch. Local restaurants may be able to accommodate you or you can gather the essentials at a grocery store.

The publicly accessible sites at Wupatki are stretched out along a north-south road paralleling Highway 89. The turnoff is well marked and you will also see a side road to Sunset

Crater shortly after you enter the park. I recommend that you bypass the Crater on your way in and go directly to the Wupatki Visitors' Center. With your entrance fee, rangers will give you a map to open sites in the Monument and provide a quick orientation. The ruins of Wupatki Pueblo are adjacent to the Visitors' Center and the ball court is strong evidence of Hohokam influence.

After you have seen the remains of Wupatki Pueblo, follow the park map to the other open sites. At the end of the day, drive back to your lodgings in Flagstaff stopping at Sunset Crater if you have the energy. Sunset views are often spectacular and the late afternoon sidelight brings out details that you might miss earlier in the day.

## DAY 3 GRAND CANYON AND TUSAYAN RUIN

Native Americans made extensive use of resources at the Grand Canyon, but relatively few ruins are open to the general public. On the other hand, it would be a shame to come so close to the Canyon without visiting.

Plan to get an early start because there is much to do and see and you will drive around 200 miles over the course of the day. Check out of your lodging, pack your car and drive north to the Grand Canyon. Tusayan Ruin is well signed as are other overlooks, and both souvenirs and lunch are readily available at a variety of shops.

At the end of the day, drive to Sedona, check into your motel, do a little shopping if you have a mind to, have a good dinner and get a good night's sleep.

## DAY 4 TUZIGOOT AND MONTEZUMA'S CASTLE

The Sinagua lived throughout the southern Verde Valley and Hohokam influence spread quickly during the 10$^{th}$ century. Today's excursion visits some of the most spectacular sites and adds the option to visit a 19$^{th}$ century "ghost town."

Start your day with a good breakfast and drive south on Highway 89 to visit Tuzigoot, about 20 miles south. The admission fee is $5 per adult and for an extra $3 you can get a combined pass that includes Montezuma's Castle, a spot we'll visit on the way back.

While you are in the area, consider adding a stop in Jerome. It's only five miles away and is a convenient spot for lunch in addition to sight seeing.

After lunch, follow highway 260/297 to the intersection with Interstate 17 and drive north to the well signed exit for Montezuma's Castle National Monument. The cliff dwelling is one of the most spectacular in the southwest and exhibits at the Visitors' Center explain who the Sinagua were and how they interacted with the Hohokam.

While you are at the Monument, be sure to get directions to Montezuma's Well and the V Bar V Petroglyph site, the final two stops on today's tour.

At the end of the day, watch for State Highway 179. It is the most direct route back to Sedona.

## DAY 5 HONONKI AND PALATKI

If you booked a jeep tour for your final day in the area, have a good breakfast and meet the tour operator.

Of course, you can visit Hononki and Palatki on your own with a Red Rock Pass and reservations. I recommend against visiting on your own because the roads are often in poor condition and there are few signs. In addition, the guides/drivers are entertaining and informative and the price is modest.

At the end of the day, return to your lodging in Sedona and enjoy a well earned rest.

## DAY 6 HOMEWARD BOUND

Your adventure has included the most important sites in the Verde Valley. Interstate Highway 40 near Flagstaff is the primary east-west route while Interstate 17 runs south to Phoenix. And, if you have more time, you can continue with the next adventure which begins near Phoenix.

# THE HOHOKAM HOP

The Hohokam dominated south central Arizona and the modern cities of Phoenix and Tucson are built on the sites of ancient villages. This tour takes advantage of well developed tourist facilities in both and includes stops at two Salado sites as well as a half dozen Hohokam sites.

If you are driving in from the north, you can add a stop at Shoofly Village near Payson by driving south on a back route, Highway 87.

Find your first night's lodging in the Miami/Globe area about 90 miles north of Phoenix.

## DAY 1 BESH BE GOWAH AND TONTO NATIONAL MONUMENT

The Salado grew up on the border of Hohokam territory and eventually replaced them in parts of their homeland. Besh be Gowah, our first stop today, reflects the transition. First occupied by the Hohokam, Besh be Gowah was abandoned for a time and then rebuilt by the Salado. Artifacts recovered at the site reflect both cultural traditions but the partially reconstructed pueblo is almost exclusively Salado. I recommend you try to be there when the site opens at 8 a.m.

From Globe it is an easy drive along Highway 188 to Tonto National Monument. Many Salado sites were destroyed by Roosevelt Dam but the two open sites in the Monument are on a hillside well above the waters of Lake Roosevelt.

At the end of the day, drive south to Phoenix about 110 miles away and find lodging for two nights. You probably won't have difficulty finding a spot, but if you would like to make reservations, see http://phoenix.lodgingguide.com/ for suggestions.

## DAY 2 HEARD MUSEUM AND PUEBLO GRANDE

Begin your day with a good breakfast and drive to the Heard Museum in the heart of downtown Phoenix. It is one of the finest museums in the southwest and you can easily entertain yourself for a half day or more. The museum café is a convenient spot for lunch.

After lunch, move on to the Pueblo Grande Museum and Archeological Park, also in Phoenix. The Museum is less substantial than the Heard but the park includes a platform mound, excavated ball court, canal segments and reconstructed Hohokam dwellings.

*A visitor takes a break at the base of the modern roof structure protecting Casa Grande Ruins. Photo by Chris Skopec*

At the end of the day, have an authentic Native American or other meal at any of the local restaurants and return to your lodgings.

## DAY 3 DEAR VALLEY ROCK ART CENTER AND LOMA DEL RIO

Day three combines sight seeing with a 60-mile drive south to Coolidge. Begin by checking out of your lodgings and packing your car. The day's highlight is a visit to the Dear Valley Rock Art Center. You can have a light breakfast at any one of the restaurants along the way, but don't tarry too long. The Dear Valley Rock Art Center is not as well known as many other spots, but its collection of Patayan and Hohokam rock art is second to none. I consider it to be a "must see" site.

Spend as much time as you like at the Center, but remember you have an hour and a half drive to your next lodging. Many people grab a quick lunch along the way and then spend an hour or two at Loma del Rio, the remains of a small Hohokam settlement in nearby Tempe.

When you are done sight seeing, find your way to Interstate Highway 17 and drive south to Coolidge. The route merges with Interstate 10 and there are a couple other wrinkles on the drive so double check your map or alert your "navigator" before you start driving.

115

Coolidge is smaller than Phoenix and its environs, but there is abundant lodging and it's a good spot to spend the night before moving on to Casa Grande.

## DAY 4 CASA GRANDE

Casa Grande is the largest and most imposing Hohokam site open to the public. The Monument's centerpiece is a massive poured adobe structure often called the "great house." The structure will probably hold your attention, but don't overlook exhibits explaining the other sites protected by the Monument.

When you finish at Casa Grande, grab a quick lunch and continue south to Tucson. The drive is just over 70 miles but it can seem longer in traffic. When you arrive, find lodging for the night, preferably along north side in the Catalina Hills area. You can find suggestions at http://tucson.lodgingguide.net/catalina_foothills_lodging.htm

## DAY 5 ROMERO RUIN AND THE HARDY SITE

Day five features visits to two unique sites. Romero Ruin is slightly less than 20 miles north of Tucson in Catalina State Park. The site is largely unexcavated and features an easy hike along a ¾ mile trail. The hike is ideal for children who are tired of being cramped up in a car, but caution them to stay on the trail because rattlesnakes also frequent the collapsed buildings.

When you finish at Romero, find a convenient spot for lunch and drive to the Hardy Site at Fort Lowell Park in downtown Tucson. The site is a fitting conclusion to your adventure because it shows the effects of subsequent development. In the 19th century, the United States Cavalry built a post over the remnants of a Hohokam village and the interpretive center displays artifacts from both occupations. More recent development encircles the park and covers a large portion of the ancient village.

At the end of the day, find convenient lodging and enjoy any of the fine restaurants in Tucson.

## DAY 6 HOMEWARD BOUND

Tucson is a major transportation hub and you should have little difficulty finding a convenient route home. If you would like to see more, check the State/Location Index for sites along your route.

# MOAB ADVENTURES

Moab is abeautiful little town in southeastern Utah. Its resident population is under 5,000 but the town hosts more than a million tourists visit every year. Most are attracted by the beautiful scenery, opportunities for mountain biking and off-roading as well as the town's proximity to Arches and Canyonlands National Parks. Visitor services are well developed and there are dozens of motels, bed and breakfasts and campgrounds. They can fill up quickly during peak season and it's a good idea to call ahead for reservations and book for 5 nights. For suggestions, check http://www.moab-utah.com

The area surrounding Moab was home to Fremont and Ancestral Puebloans as well as earlier peoples. Rock art is abundant and you will encounter a fair number of abandoned dwellings, especially when you drive south on the final day of this adventure.

116

One word of warning; the area surrounding Moab is sparsely populated and services are scarce outside the city. Be sure to fill your fuel tank and stock up on water and snacks every day before you go.

## DAY 1 MOAB ROCK ART SITES

Many rock art panels are near roads and today you can visit the Golf Course Rock Art Site, Kane Creek Road Rock Art Sites, Highway 279 Rock Art Sites, Courthouse Wash Rock Art Site and the Buckhorn Wash Rock Art Site. Each of them is described in the alphabetic listing and you can download a helpful brochure from http://discovermoab. com/rockart.htm.

## DAY 2 ARCHES NATIONAL PARK

Arches National Park is just 5 miles north Moab. Archaic and Fremont people ventured into the area protected by the park as did Ancestral Puebloans. All gathered stone for tools and lived in temporary shelters. Scattered rock art, broken ceramics and lithic scatters are unmistakable signs of their presence.

You can see many of the arches for which the park is named on short walks from your car. Park service personnel will be pleased to help you find other sites of interest and it is easy to spend a full day at Arches. I usually pack a light meal and find a shaded overlook to eat my lunch.

At the end of the day, return to your lodgings in Moab.

## DAY 3 CANYONLANDS, ISLAND IN THE SKY

Canyonlands National Park is noted for it natural beauty and extensive rock art collections. The park is divided into three units and today's adventure visits the Island in the Sky District, 32 miles from Moab.

Aztec Butte Ruins are a very short walk from a parking area and helpful rangers will give you directions to other easily accessible sites. Again, this is a good day for a picnic lunch and you can return to Moab when you are done for the day.

## DAY 4 CANYONLANDS, NEEDLES AND NEWSPAPER ROCK

The Needles District is 55 miles from Moab but your drive includes a stop at Newspaper Rock. One of the most famous sites in the area, Newspaper Rock is a large boulder covered with Archaic, Fremont and Ancestral Puebloan glyphs. The site is now a State Historic Monument and the turnoff is well signed.

In the Needles Unit, be sure to visit Roadside Ruin and ask rangers about other sites of interest. Again, bring a picnic lunch and return to your lodgings in Moab at the end of the day.

## DAY 5 EDGE OF THE CEDARS

Begin your day by checking out of your lodgings and have a good breakfast. Your next stop is in Blanding, about 75 miles south on Highway 191.

Edge of the Cedars State Park centers on a partially excavated and reconstructed Pueblo. The visible remnant is smaller and cruder than others you may see, but the museum

*Double Arch in Arches National Park. National Park Service photo*

is among the best in the southwest. Pay particular attention to wooden and fiber artifacts that have survived in dry caves in the immediate area.

Have a pleasant lunch and decide how you would like to spend the afternoon. Mule Canyon, Cave Towers and Butler Wash ruins are all nearby. Bluff, Utah is just 25 miles away and you can find lodging there for the final night of this adventure.

### DAY 6 HOMEWARD BOUND

Bluff is hardly a transportation hub, but state highways connect with larger towns and more developed transportation facilities. Cortez, Colorado only 100 miles away and Flagstaff, Arizona is about twice as far. If you feel like visiting more sites, Hovenweep National Monument is an easy drive from Bluff and the Sand Island Petroglyph is even closer. And, if you would like to shop for souvenirs or meet the Ancestral Puebloans' descendents, the Hopi Mesas are just about 125 miles from Bluff.

# INDEXES

*Broken Walls of Pueblo Bonito in Chaco Culture National Historic Park. For more on Pueblo Bonito, see page 78 and page 30 (Chaco Culture National Historical Park). Photo by Chris Skopec*

## SECTIONS

# MUST-SEE SITES

This short list of "must see" sites includes all of the three handprint sites described in the second chapter. They are all so important that visiting them is essential if you want to understand the anciet southwest. All of these sites are well developed for visitation and you will have little difficulty finding nearby services.

# LOCATION INDEX

Use this index to quickly locate sites of interest near you whenever you are in the southwest. The list excludes zero handprint sites that are difficult to visit and double lists sites that cross state borders. For example, Hovenweep straddles the Utah Colorado border and is listed with proximate cities in both states.

## ARIZONA

## Colorado

## New Mexico

# CULTURE INDEX

This index list sites alphabetically by the culture that created them. Sites that were occupied by more than one culture are listed in each.

## ANCESTRAL PUEBLOAN

## Archaic

## Fremont

## Hohokam

## MIMBRES

## MOGOLLON

## NAVAJO

## PATAYAN

## SALADO

## SINAGUA

# INDEX OF MUSEUMS, ASSOCIATIONS, & FOUNDATIONS

Made in the USA
Charleston, SC
04 June 2010